DISCOVER RECOVERY

DISCOVER RECOVERY

A Comprehensive Addiction Recovery Workbook

Central Recovery

CENTRAL RECOVERY PRESS

LAS VEGAS

Central Recovery Press (CRP) is committed to publishing exceptional materials addressing addiction treatment, recovery, and behavioral healthcare topics.

For more information, visit www.centralrecoverypress.com.

Publisher: Central Recovery Press
              3321 N Buffalo Drive
              Las Vegas, NV 89129

22 21 20 19 18 17   1 2 3 4 5

Library of Congress Cataloging-in-Publication Data

LC record available at https://lccn.loc.gov/2016058860

Every attempt has been made to contact copyright holders. If copyright holders have not been properly acknowledged please contact us. Central Recovery Press will be happy to rectify the omission in future printings of this book.

Some of the information on the Four Points of Balance was adapted from *Pain Recovery: How to Find Balance and Reduce Suffering from Chronic Pain* by Pohl, Szabo, Shiode, and Hunter (Central Recovery Press, 2009).

Publisher's Note: This guidebook contains general information about the disease of addiction and the process of recovery. Every effort has been made to ensure that events, institutions, and statistics presented in our books as facts are accurate and up-to-date. Central Recovery Press makes no representations or warranties in relation to the information herein; it is not an alternative to professional treatment or medical advice from your doctor or other professional healthcare provider.

Cover design and interior by Sara Streifel, Think Creative Design

TABLE OF CONTENTS

This work is dedicated to
everyone on the path of recovery
and those who may yet
find their way to it.

INTRODUCTION

Recovery from active addiction is extremely challenging, even under the best of circumstances. Understanding the recovery process and the issues closely connected to it can be especially confusing for people who are in treatment or new to recovery. However, both research and experience demonstrate that treatment works and recovery is possible.

Because addiction is a condition that affects people mentally, emotionally, physically, and spiritually, *Discover Recovery* presents a holistic approach to recovery that includes mental, emotional, physical, and spiritual components—the Four Points of Balance. Recovery requires achieving and maintaining balance among these four life domains, as well as within each of them.

Discover Recovery is based on the philosophy that recovery truly occurs when people make changes internally. Recovery involves becoming aware of problematic patterns of thinking; developing the capacity to tolerate distressing feeling states; and replacing self-defeating behaviors with healthy, growth-enhancing ways of relating to oneself, to others, and to the world. External factors, such as living environment, family and social relationships, finances, employment status, and legal entanglements, also have obvious importance, and abstinence requires making changes with regard to specific "people, places, and things" associated with an individual's active addiction.

Recovery is a function of the dialectical relationship between the individual's internal and external circumstances. These two elements, "inside" and "outside," are in continuous interface, exerting influence on one another. In early recovery there are many serious challenges that can make the path of recovery seem like a steep uphill hike. Consider *Discover Recovery* as a guide that provides the equipment to assist you on your recovery journey. This equipment consists of information and maps to guide you through rough, uneven, and potentially dangerous terrain. This material will also provide you with tools and help you learn the skills necessary to overcome obstacles you will encounter along the way.

When you struggle with addiction, everything you experience and how you react to those experiences has the potential to either strengthen your recovery or pull you back toward active addiction. *Discover Recovery* includes the following sections, structured to help you identify challenges and give you the awareness, strategies, and solutions that can help you build and maintain your recovery:

• Addiction and Its Manifestations

• Roadblocks to Recovery

• Pathways to Recovery

• Trauma, Addiction, and Recovery

• Addiction as a Family Disease

This approach to recovery is strengths-based and research-informed. It integrates current neuroscience on addiction and recovery; the time-tested principles of twelve-step recovery; elements of mindfulness; and aspects of the evidence-based approaches of cognitive-behavioral therapy (CBT), Acceptance and Commitment Therapy (ACT), and Dialectical Behavior Therapy (DBT). This unique synthesis is designed to help readers develop greater understanding of how thoughts, beliefs, emotions, and actions are interconnected, expand their awareness of the choices inherent in every situation, and construct the skills to respond in intentional and healthier ways.

> In order to be successful in any process of meaningful change,
> both awareness and action are necessary.

Through the exercises provided, readers can develop the capacity to observe, question, and challenge thoughts; better tolerate and accept painful emotions and physical sensations instead of numbing or running from them; and respond to the situation at hand consciously as opposed to reacting automatically based on past conditioning.

In order to be successful in any process of meaningful change, both awareness and action are necessary. Without an awareness of your current status (where you are now) and your goal(s) (where you want to be), your actions will often be without direction and ineffective, wasting precious time and energy. So awareness is important, but awareness by itself rarely results in change—only doing things differently leads to change.

Translating awareness into action in recovery from addiction is similar to the process of building new skills in any area, be it sports, cooking, auto repair, reading, keyboarding, gardening, painting, plumbing, or meditating. In order to get better at anything it is necessary to 1) **learn** what works, and 2) **practice** what works with consistency and persistence, even (or perhaps, especially) when you may not feel like it.

NOTES

_____

_____

_____

_____

_____

_____

_____

_____

_____

ADDICTION AND ITS MANIFESTATIONS

What Is Addiction?

Exactly what is meant by the term, addiction? The approach of this workbook is that addiction is one disease with many manifestations. Addiction can take many different forms and includes activities, as well as substances. All forms of the disease of addiction share certain universal characteristics, as well as progressive and predictable negative consequences.

Previously, the fields of research and treatment have divided addiction into separate categories for substance addiction and process (activity) addiction. Substance addiction has been subdivided according to specific drugs—alcohol, heroin/opiates/opioids, cocaine, methamphetamine, marijuana, tranquilizers, sedatives, etc.—while process addiction has been subdivided based on the particular activity involved—gambling, eating, sex, pornography, shopping/spending, Internet use, video gaming, etc.

This traditional perspective makes it seem as though there are many different types of addiction and suggests that one person can potentially have a variety of addictions. It downplays similarities and focuses on differences, even though the underlying similarities far outweigh any surface differences.

Because these various manifestations of addiction are so intimately connected, it is much more useful to address addiction as one illness. As a result, when **using** is referred to in this workbook, it means the use of any substance or activity. For example, if your addiction manifests in gambling, then playing blackjack, poker, roulette, or slots is considered using.

**ADDICTION IS ONE DISEASE
WITH MANY MANIFESTATIONS**

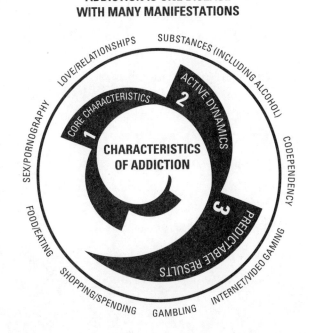

All of these forms (manifestations) of the disease of addiction change how the brain works in similar ways. They all share the same facilitating factors and active dynamics, as well as predictable negative consequences.

I. CORE CHARACTERISTICS

- **Internal Emptiness:** This is a sense or feeling of being empty, hollow, or missing something. The specific manifestation(s) of addiction—be it a substance or an activity—is an attempt to fill this hole.

- **Sense of Self as "Different" or as "Not Fitting In:"** This is a deep-seated experience of oneself as being separate from or unlike others; of feeling alone no matter how many people are around; of being "on the outside looking in." Using becomes a way to temporarily block out or soften this sense of being different and creates a connection with others who use.

- **Emotional Hypersensitivity/Inability to Tolerate Uncomfortable, Painful Feelings:** This is a heightened sensitivity where emotions are felt more deeply and rapidly than in most other people. As a result, distressing emotions, including anxiety, fear, anger, sadness, depression, as well as physical pain are not only felt with pronounced intensity, they are often experienced as overwhelming, almost suffocating. Using becomes a way to turn down the volume of such feelings and to numb them in order to endure them.

These core characteristics create a vulnerability to addiction for people before they ever come in contact with alcohol and/or other drugs, gambling, sex, pornography, Internet use, video gaming, or any other potential "object" of addiction. Whenever this personal predisposition to addiction is combined with mood-altering substances and/or activities, it is the equivalent of lighting an old-style fuse on a stick of dynamite.

II. ACTIVE DYNAMICS

- **Discomfort/Pain Avoidance:** This is characterized by attempts to avoid distressing thoughts, feelings, memories, physical sensations, and other internal experiences, through the use of substances and/or activities. Because avoidance through using achieves short-term relief of discomfort, using behavior is reinforced and continues.

- **Obsession:** This is a persistent preoccupation with, thinking about, and desire for the specific manifestation(s) of addiction. Obsession is one of the **mental/emotional** components of addiction.

- **Compulsion:** This is an irresistible impulse to act on the obsession for the specific manifestation(s) of addiction. Compulsion is one of the **physical/behavioral** components of addiction.

- **Self-Centeredness:** This is a self-absorbed pursuit of the manifestation(s) of addiction that focuses on one's own desires, feelings, and perceived needs to the neglect of consideration of consequences and the needs of others. Self-centeredness is one of the **spiritual** components of addiction.

- **Withdrawal:** This is the experience of mental, emotional, and/or physical distress or discomfort when use of the specific manifestation(s) of addiction is discontinued activating the drive for discomfort/pain avoidance.

If the core characteristics mixed with one or more of the objects of addiction ignite the fuse, then these active dynamics are what propel the spark along the fuse toward the dynamite; sometimes the fuse is long and takes more time to burn until the dynamite explodes, and sometimes it's short and takes little time until it all blows up.

III. PREDICTABLE RESULTS

- **Progression:** This refers to the escalation of the disease of addiction as it increases in intensity, frequency, and severity. Over time, active addiction consumes a greater percentage of time, attention, and energy. It always leads to problems in different areas of life, and those problems will become more and more serious.

- **Loss of Control:** This is characterized by the inability to limit the amount and frequency of use of the specific manifestation(s) of addiction.

- **Continuing Use Despite Increasingly Serious Negative Consequences:** These consequences include, but are not limited to problems and losses related to family, relationships, health, employment, finances, and other interests.

These negative consequences are the predictable results of the spark reaching the dynamite and exploding. The explosion usually leaves serious wreckage in its wake, affecting the lives of not only the individual struggling with addiction, but all those who are close to him or her.

Denial and other defense mechanisms are interwoven with all of the above-mentioned aspects of addiction. Denial is both an active dynamic of addiction and a predictable result of it. Denial convinces addicts that they do not have the disease of addiction and enables them to continue to use despite worsening problems. It is a natural and unconscious form of self-protection that clouds a person's ability to accurately identify obsession, compulsion, and self-centeredness, and thus admit addiction. An addict may deny his or her addiction, the extent of his or her use, and the problems it creates because the reality is too uncomfortable and painful. In this way, denial functions as another layer of distress avoidance.

Describe your experience with the Core Characteristics of addiction.

Internal Emptiness

_____

_____

_____

_____

Sense of Self as "Different" or as "Not Fitting In"

_____

_____

_____

_____

Emotional Hypersensitivity/Inability to Tolerate Uncomfortable, Painful Feelings

_____

_____

_____

_____

To paraphrase the definition by the American Society of Addiction Medicine (ASAM)*:

> Addiction is a primary, chronic disease of brain reward, motivation, memory, and related circuitry. Addiction is characterized by impairment in behavioral control, craving, inability to consistently abstain, and diminished recognition of significant problems with one's behaviors and interpersonal relationships. Without treatment or engagement in recovery activities, addiction is progressive and can result in disability or premature death.

This brain dysfunction leads to characteristic biological, psychological, social, and spiritual effects that include impairments in emotional response and behavioral control, craving, and inability to consistently abstain, along with diminished recognition of significant problems with one's behaviors and interpersonal relationships.

Addiction evolves from an unhealthy and mood-altering relationship between a person and the manifestation(s) of his or her addiction, whether substances—drugs that can be used to change how a person feels, regardless of whether these drugs come from the street (cocaine/crack, heroin/opiates, meth/speed, marijuana, hallucinogens) or are prescribed by a doctor (painkillers, tranquilizers, sedatives) or are bought at a store (alcohol, over-the-counter medications, and other substances, such as inhalants)—or activities (gambling, eating, shopping/spending, sex, pornography, Internet use, video gaming, love/relationships, etc.) to the point where using the substance or engaging in the activity becomes beyond voluntary control and continues regardless of increasingly negative consequences.

From this perspective, codependency is one of the many manifestations of the disease of addiction. The feeling that people struggling with addiction experience of not being able to survive without cocaine, alcohol, opiates, or pot is the same feeling someone who is codependent experiences related to another person. It is essentially the same process as the addict who *must* gamble, *must* have sex, *must* shop/spend money, *must* eat more, *must* play video games or go online, *must* be in a primary relationship, or *must* take care of others.

WHAT CAUSES ADDICTION?

While research indicates there is a genetic predisposition toward addiction, a predisposition is not the same as a predetermination. A predisposition increases the risk of something occurring, but it cannot by itself cause it to happen. Another key factor is the environment. Genes are activated or turned off by the environment. Whether a person becomes addicted is often influenced by a variety of factors including genetics/biology, family history of addiction, quality of family relationships, childhood experiences, mental health, exposure to physical or sexual abuse or other kinds of trauma, or the degree of drug use/addiction in one's social circles, neighborhood, and community.

(*The complete definition of addiction may be found on the ASAM website: asam.org/for-the-public/definition-of-addiction.)

In active addiction, the need to use substances or engage in other activities becomes so strong that it overrides most all other needs and creates problems that only get worse over time. The object of addiction, regardless of whether it is a substance or an activity, becomes the highest priority and assumes greater importance than family, friends, health, and work.

It becomes the organizing focus in the lives of addicts, taking over their attention, time, and energy. As a result, addicts are often driven to sacrifice what they previously cherished most in order to preserve and continue to live in their active addiction.

> The object of addiction, regardless of whether it is a substance or an activity, becomes the highest priority and assumes more importance than family, friends, health, and work.

At first, most people experience initial positive effects by using drugs or activities to change the way they feel. They experience the reward of feeling "good" and/or the relief of feeling "better." Mind- and mood-altering substances and activities provide a way to temporarily avoid or lessen feelings of emotional or physical discomfort, such as anxiety, depression, anger, physical pain, fear, boredom, and/or stress. Stress can play a major role in beginning involvement with drugs and/or activities, continuing involvement, or for people in recovery, relapse into active addiction.

Those who become addicted almost always believe they can control their using, even after there is plenty of evidence that the use of substances or participation in activities has taken over their lives. In this way, denial and other defense mechanisms that are characteristic of the disease of addiction, such as minimization and rationalization, convince those who suffer from it that they do not have it.

Defense mechanisms are unconscious psychological processes that come into play outside of your awareness to help you cope with painful aspects of reality. This process can happen quickly—sometimes in a matter of days or weeks or unfold gradually over several months or even years. When drug use or participation in the activities previously noted continues over time, other interests that were important and pleasurable, such as recreational activities and hobbies, relationships with family and friends, work, health, etc., become less important and less pleasurable. More and more time and energy are spent thinking about, pursuing, and participating in the manifestations of addiction, as well as facing the aftermath of its consequences, such as withdrawal, hangovers, injuries, missed responsibilities, and financial problems.

Addicts reach a point where they are driven to continue their involvement with the manifestations of their addiction despite the problems it creates for both themselves and their loved ones.

HOW ADDICTION AFFECTS YOUR BRAIN

As both ASAM and National Institute on Drug Abuse (NIDA) have declared, addiction is a brain disease. Neuroscience increasingly demonstrates that repetitive experiences effectively shape the brain. The use of substances and mood-altering activities changes brain structure and functioning, directly altering how it sends and receives information. The brain uses a communication system that sends and receives messages through certain naturally occurring chemicals, called **neurotransmitters**. The research is crystal clear; substance use effectively hijacks the brain's reward system by changing the levels of specific neurotransmitters. Think of the reward system on steroids or other performance enhancers.

When the reward system, located deep within a part of the brain known as the limbic system, is activated through messages sent by particular neurotransmitters, people experience pleasure. Research on the brain's reward system indicates that a reward is a reward, regardless of whether it comes from a drug or an activity.

> At one time, people who are addicted made a decision to use;
> however, they did not make a decision to become addicted.

Activities such as gambling, eating, sex/pornography, shopping/spending, Internet use, and video gaming also stimulate the release of neurotransmitters that activate the reward system in the brain. It is this stimulation of the brain's reward system that produces the mood-changing effects sought by people through the use of drugs and participation in activities. Basically, you learn through the experience of using how you can give yourself a dose of pleasure.

Your brain is in charge of your body's basic functions and gives you the ability to interpret and respond to everything you experience. In this way, your brain directs the course of your thoughts, emotions, and behaviors. At one time, people who are addicted made a decision to use; however, they did not make a decision to become addicted. No one intends to become addicted. At first, the decision to use is a conscious choice, but as addiction progressively alters brain functioning and takes over a person's life, he or she loses more and more of the ability to exercise control over his or her thoughts, impulses, choices, and actions.

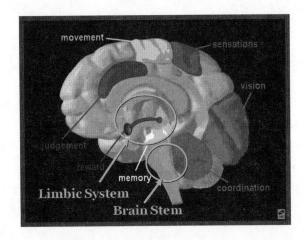

Brain imaging studies provide evidence that addicts experience physical changes in the areas of their brains that involve judgment, decision-making, learning and memory, and behavior control. These changes affect how the brain works in important ways. They help to explain the cycle of obsessive thinking, compulsive behaviors, and self-centeredness (including the decreased capacity to consider the consequences of choices and behaviors), in which addiction traps those who struggle with it. Addiction erodes a person's capacity for self-control as well as the ability to make healthy decisions. This only gets worse over time as addiction drives the need to continue to use more to try to recreate the intense pleasure of the highs and avoid the devastating lows of the crash of withdrawal.

The brain adapts to repetitive experiences by forming memory connections or tracks that are unconscious. These unconscious memory tracks are the foundation of the "habits" of addiction. Such habits can be difficult to control because they are created by changes in the brain's operating system, outside of conscious awareness. The powerful desire addicts experience for their drug or activity, sometimes long after they last used, is an example of the strength of these memory tracks.

Positive reinforcement, the desired outcome that results from using, for example, feeling "good" or "better," is one form of this process. And each time using results in the desired outcome, the memory track between the manifestation(s) of addiction and the result becomes stronger. This positive reinforcement teaches you to repeat the same behaviors in order to get the same results. The more you repeat it, the greater the chances are that you will continue to repeat it, as the vicious circle of addiction intensifies.

Conditioning is another example of how the brain adapts to repeated experiences. Certain emotional states (anger, depression, anxiety, fear, etc.) and situations, including specific people and places, become connected with the experience of using and can light the fire of obsessive thoughts, compulsive behaviors, and self-centered tunnel-vision. This unconscious learned response is strong enough that it can occur even after years of abstinence. As a result, these memory tracks tend to pull people back toward the experiences and behaviors with which they are familiar and comfortable, making it more difficult to stop such behaviors and stay stopped.

> The brain adapts to repetitive experiences by forming memory connections or tracks that are unconscious.

Over time, your brain also adjusts to these changes so it takes more and more of a drug or activity to get the same effect. This is known as **tolerance**. Sooner or later, tolerance develops, and because of it, the object of addiction becomes less and less effective in giving you the results you are seeking. All addicts eventually reach a point where using is no longer "fun," it has become "work," something you "have" to do. You rarely get "high" anymore, and use solely to try to feel "normal" or what has become normal for you.

ADDICTION IS ADDICTION

> Habits—patterns of behavior that develop through repetition—are both a cause, as well as a result of changes in the brain.

As previously described, addiction in all its manifestations begins with mood-changing effects that initially help to make people feel "good" or "better," and can seem to temporarily ease, numb, or block out life's problems. However, when using turns into an ongoing way to cope with life's stresses and challenges, and becomes a primary coping strategy, it is no longer voluntary—addiction has taken control. In other words, the relationship with the object of addiction has progressed to the point where it is beyond a person's ability to control it and their life becomes increasingly unmanageable.

Addiction has certain characteristics that separate the "addict" from the "nonaddict." The obsessive thinking combined with compulsive behaviors and self-centeredness that come to control an addict's life create powerful habits. In fact, potentially addictive medications have warnings that they may be "habit-forming." Habits—patterns of behavior that develop through repetition—are both a cause, as well as a result of changes in the brain.

Any repetitive behavior or experience, but especially those with mood-changing effects such as alcohol or other drug use and participation in certain activities, can create new unconscious memory tracks. The formation of these memory tracks in the brain is like the grading and paving of a roadway that allows traffic to travel easily and efficiently. Over time, repetitive use of drugs or activities can turn an unpaved one-lane road into a multi-lane freeway.

Because addiction is addiction, once you are addicted to any drug, including alcohol, you are automatically at much greater risk of your addiction shifting to another drug or activity, such as gambling, eating, sex, shopping/spending, Internet use, and video gaming. This is true even if you are in recovery.

When you are addicted to any substance, crack cocaine for example, you are at an extremely high risk for your addiction to cross over to alcohol or prescription pain medications or marijuana or any other substance you use. You may think, *I've never had a problem with alcohol, so I can have a drink*, or that *Pot is no big deal*, or that *Percocet/Vicodin/Lortab/Xanax/etc. must be okay for me to take because a doctor prescribed it.*

Place a "C" next to those you use currently; an "R" next to those you used most recently; and a "P" next to those you have used in the past.

_____ Heroin/opiates	_____ Prescription pain meds	_____ Cocaine/crack
_____ Methamphetamine	_____ Alcohol	_____ Marijuana
_____ Tobacco	_____ Sedatives (sleeping meds)	_____ Hallucinogens
_____ Inhalants	_____ Tranquilizers (Xanax, Valium, Klonopin)	

Others (please list) _____

_____

In the same way, your inner voice may say, "I know I can't use, but I can go spend a bunch of money shopping," or "Go gambling," because "there's no harm in those activities." Substituting one manifestation of addiction for another is similar to switching where you are sitting on a boat that is sinking—you may be able to stay dry for a little longer, but you will still end up in the water, with all of the potential dangers that go with it.

When experienced in moderation (in a balanced way), many of the activities listed below are simply part of life and can even be healthy up to a point. However, people can get caught up in these activities in ways that are obsessive, compulsive, and self-centered. They all have the potential to be used excessively and as external "fixes" for the internal emptiness that addiction attempts to fill. People may try to "fix" with these activities, using them to change the way they feel—to feel better (e.g., fill the emptiness) or feel different (e.g., redirect emotions).

Place a "C" next to those you use currently; an "R" next to those you used most recently; and a "P" next to those you have used as a fix in the past:

_____ Gambling	_____ Sex	_____ Shopping/spending
_____ Pornography	_____ Food/eating	_____ Love/relationships
_____ Internet use	_____ Video gaming	_____ Fantasy sports

Others (please list) _____

_____

Answer each of the following questions as honestly as you can. Please keep in mind that **using** refers to any substance or activity.

☐ **At times I have used or engaged in more or for a longer period of time than I intended.**

EXAMPLE: *I said I was only going to take two Lortabs, but ended up taking four and drinking a couple of Bloody Marys.*

Describe a situation when you ended up using more or using for a longer period of time than you intended.

_____

_____

_____

☐ **I have stopped or cut back on social, recreation, work, or other activities because of my using.**

Example: *I haven't seen my parents in over a month because I'm always at the casino on weekends.*

Describe how your using has affected your participation in social, recreational, and other activities.

_____

_____

_____

☐ **I have used more or for longer periods to try to get the same high, feeling, or effect.**

Describe how you had to use more or for longer periods to try to get the same high, feeling, or effect.

_____

_____

_____

☐ **I have thought about cutting down or tried to limit/control my using or *tried* to quit.**

Describe a situation when you tried to cut down how much you used or how often you used or tried to quit using entirely.

_____

_____

_____

☐ **I have continued using despite negative consequences to my (check all that apply):**

○ **Self-esteem**

How has using affected the way you feel about yourself?

_____

_____

_____

List the specific manifestations of addiction that were involved.

_____

_____

○ **Family**

How has using affected your family?

_____

_____

_____

List the specific manifestations of addiction that were involved.

_____

_____

○ **Mood**

How has using affected your mood?

_____

_____

_____

List the specific manifestations of addiction that were involved.

_____

_____

○ **Relationships**

How has using affected your relationships?

_____

_____

_____

List the specific manifestations of addiction that were involved.

_____

_____

○ **Work**

How has using affected your work or your ability to work?

_____

_____

_____

List the specific manifestations of addiction that were involved.

_____

_____

○ **School**

How has using affected your school work and attendance?

_____

_____

_____

List the specific manifestations of addiction that were involved.

_____

_____

○ **Health**

How has using affected your health?

_____

_____

_____

List the specific manifestations of addiction that were involved.

_____

_____

○ **Legal status**

How has using affected you legally?

_____

_____

_____

Describe how much time you spend planning, getting, or using in an average day.

_____

_____

_____

List the specific manifestations of addiction that are involved.

_____

_____

Describe how much time you spend recovering from the effects of using in an average day.

_____

_____

_____

List the specific manifestations of addiction that are involved.

_____

_____

When I don't use I experience the following (check all that apply):

○ Sweating   ○ Nausea   ○ Vomiting   ○ Diarrhea

○ Anxiety   ○ Depression   ○ Irritability   ○ Headaches

○ Anger   ○ Shaking/tremors   ○ Seizures   ○ Insomnia

○ Lack of appetite   ○ Chills/fever   ○ Aches/pain

○ Lack of energy/listlessness

Describe what happens to you physically and emotionally when you don't or can't use.

_____

_____

_____

OBSESSION, COMPULSION, SELF-CENTEREDNESS, AND DENIAL

Obsession is the primary mental component of addiction and involves recurring and persistent thoughts about using. Obsession is thinking about something, such as using, over and over and over, like a song stuck on repeat that won't stop playing.

> **Obsession** is the primary mental component of addiction and involves recurring and persistent thoughts about using.

When you are actively obsessed with any manifestation of addiction, it can be difficult to think about anything else. If you think about using long enough, chances are you will eventually act on those thoughts and end up using.

Which of the manifestations of addiction that you previously listed do you obsess over currently?

_____

_____

Which of the manifestations of addiction that you previously listed have you obsessed over in the past?

_____

_____

Describe how obsession works as related to your using.

_____

_____

_____

Describe in detail the thought process you had before you last used.

_____

_____

_____

When you are obsessed with something, you cannot see where this thought process will take you or where it will end up. Give an example of how your obsessive thinking took you to a place you did not expect.

_____

_____

_____

_____

If you were to watch yourself on a video screen when you are caught up in obsessive thinking, describe in detail what you would see.

_____

_____

_____

Describe the feelings you have when you are obsessed with something.

_____

_____

When you are actively using, what percentage of the day do you spend thinking about using?

_____

_____

What percentage of the day do you think about using now (include thinking about your past use)?

_____

_____

Compulsion is the primary physical or behavioral aspect of addiction. Compulsion is an overwhelming impulse to act on an obsession. You feel like you *have* to do it, as if you are being driven to do it by forces beyond your control. The behavior or action always follows the thought. Two of the defining conditions of addiction are continued use despite negative consequences and loss of control over the amount used. Compulsive use is using any manifestation of addiction even when you do not want to use—even when you promised yourself that you were not going to use and even though you may have told yourself and others that you were going to quit using.

> **Compulsion** is the primary physical or behavioral aspect of addiction.

Once you start using, the full intensity of your addiction is unleashed as the changes in your brain chemistry kick in, and the compulsion to continue to use can take over your behavior and drive you to use over and over again. This process will happen no matter how often you tell yourself that you can control your use or that it will somehow be "different this time."

Which of the manifestations of addiction you previously listed have you acted compulsively with?

_____

_____

Which of the manifestations of addiction you previously listed are you most at risk to act compulsively with?

_____

_____

Describe how compulsion works in your using.

_____

_____

_____

Describe three situations when you used more than you intended to.

1. _____

_____

2. _____

_____

3. _____

_____

Describe your feelings after you used more than you intended to.

_____

_____

_____

If you were to watch yourself on a video screen when you are acting compulsively, describe in detail what you would see.

_____

_____

_____

Describe three examples of attempts you have made to either control your use or to stop using.

1. _____

_____

_____

2. _____

_____

_____

3. _____

_____

_____

Describe three examples when you substituted one manifestation of addiction for another, thinking that somehow it would be different.

1. _____

_____

_____

2. _____

_____

_____

3. _____

_____

_____

Self-centeredness is the primary spiritual aspect of addiction. Spirituality requires a sense of connection to something greater than oneself, which may or may not be related to formal religious beliefs. Spirituality involves experiencing a positive connection to others and to the world around you, a feeling of belonging to a greater whole. In contrast, self-centeredness is thinking and acting as if the world revolves around you, and that your desires, wishes, needs, and feelings are more important than those of other people. Put simply, it's all about you. Self-centeredness is a self-absorbed pursuit of the manifestations of addiction regardless of the consequences. The self-centeredness of addiction results in a tunnel-vision-like focus on using and finding all sorts of ways to continue to use.

> **Self-centeredness** is the primary spiritual aspect of addiction.

Self-centeredness cultivates an attitude of immediate gratification—getting what you want when you want it, which usually translates to "right now, if not sooner." Self-centeredness also often makes it difficult for addicts to see and understand how they contribute to their own problems because in their distorted thinking other people and institutions are almost always to blame.

Which of the manifestations of addiction you previously listed have you acted most self-centered with?

_____

_____

Which of the manifestations of addiction you previously listed are you most at risk to act self-centered with?

_____

_____

Describe how self-centeredness works in your using.

_____

_____

_____

Describe three situations when you specifically tried NOT to act in self-centered ways, but did anyway as part of your using.

1. _____

_____

_____

2. _____

_____

_____

3. _____

_____

_____

Describe how your self-centeredness has affected other people in your life.

_____

_____

_____

Describe your feelings after you act in self-centered ways.

_____

_____

_____

Describe how you blame other people and institutions for problems you have experienced.

_____

_____

_____

If you were to watch yourself on a video screen when you are caught up in self-centeredness, describe in detail what you would see.

_____

_____

_____

Describe how your priorities and values have changed as a result of your self-centered thoughts and behaviors.

_____

_____

_____

One definition of insanity is to do the same thing over and over expecting the results will be different: "I know the last ten times I did *this*, the result was *that*. But this time, I simply know it will be different." This also is known as wishful thinking and can be a form of the defense mechanism of denial.

> People in denial seem to ignore unpleasant facts and simply reject information that contradicts what they need to believe.

Denial goes hand-in-hand with addiction. People in denial seem to ignore unpleasant facts and simply reject information that contradicts what they need to believe. For those struggling with addiction, denial most often involves refusing to admit they have a problem because that reality creates too much anxiety, stress, or pain. Thinking addiction *won't happen to me* is another form of denial. Even after you become aware that you have the disease of addiction and begin a process of recovery, denial can reemerge. Because you tend to feel better after the drugs are out of your system, denial may come back and try to convince you that you no longer have a problem much less a disease.

Denial influences you to believe you can control your using and that you do not suffer with addiction no matter how much evidence may be present. Even when everyone close to you can clearly see your life spiraling out of control, denial can keep you convinced your biggest problem is that these people won't leave you alone, and that if everyone would just stop nagging you everything would be okay. Even when you can muster the strength and courage to admit your using is beyond your ability to control it and you are powerless over it, denial can keep you from accepting the fact that in order to recover you need help and that you cannot do it alone. After all, if you could do this by yourself you would have!

Your denial may even be talking to you right now, whispering in your ear, trying to convince you that this is all nonsense and you actually don't need any help at all. Denial is often confused with dishonesty. It is important to be aware that the unconscious process of denial—being unable to accept and admit the truth because it's so painful—is notably different from dishonesty or lying. Lying is when you know the truth and yet choose to make statements you know are false or misleading.

Describe two examples of how denial has played a role in your addiction.

1. _____

_____

_____

2. _____

_____

_____

If you were to watch yourself on a video screen when you have been in denial related to your addiction, describe in detail what you would see.

_____

_____

_____

If denial were to reemerge during your recovery, what do you think it would look like?

_____

_____

_____

Stimulating and pleasure-seeking experiences are used to fill one up and to try to feel whole while keeping feelings of discomfort, distress, and *dis-ease* at a distance. Whatever pleasure one finds by using and however long it lasts is always followed by even greater *dis-ease* that is fueled by the depletion of the neurotransmitters the brain needs to maintain a "normal" mood, along with the guilt, remorse, and shame that naturally accompany the negative consequences of addiction in progress.

As a disease, addiction is a chronic, progressive, and potentially fatal illness, similar to other chronic life-threatening diseases such as Type 2 diabetes, asthma, and heart disease. Like these other diseases, there is no cure for addiction. However, it can be treated and managed successfully through the process of recovery, allowing those who are afflicted with it to live long, full, and healthy lives.

> As a disease, addiction is a chronic, progressive, and potentially fatal illness, similar to other chronic life-threatening diseases such as Type 2 diabetes, asthma, and heart disease.

What Is Recovery?

Addiction is treatable, and the majority of its impact on the brain is reversible by maintaining abstinence and the process of recovery. This has been confirmed through scientific research using brain imaging. As a result of neuroplasticity—the human brain's lifelong ability to adapt to changing experiences by growing new neurons and developing new neuronal pathways—recovery-supportive experiences actually heal the brain. The integration of new coping skills and healthy patterns of living is made possible by this ability of the brain to make structural and functional changes. Over time, our brains become actual reflections of our actions, knowledge, and skills.

> It takes strength and courage to do anything that is uncomfortable.

Beyond abstinence, recovery is an ongoing process of learning, growing, and healing—mentally, emotionally, physically, and spiritually. It involves coming to terms with oneself as one truly is, and accepting life on its own terms with its full range of pain and pleasure, while expanding the capacity to act intentionally with awareness rather than react habitually and reflexively. It is about making conscious decisions consistent with what each person values most and taking action to spend their available energy and precious time in ways that accurately reflect their priorities.

Recovery requires abstinence from drugs, including alcohol, and addictive behaviors. However, it involves much more than abstinence, recovery is about learning how to live a whole, healthy, and healed life.

There are important differences between **abstinence** and **recovery.**

- **Abstinence** is when a person avoids the object(s) of his or her addiction, whether drugs, and/or activities. In the case of activities where total abstinence is neither possible nor healthy, such as eating and sex, the focus is on avoiding problematic involvement and developing balance.

- Being in **recovery** means a person is abstinent from the object(s) of his or her addiction *and* is also participating in life activities that are healthy, meaningful, and fulfilling.

- With recovery, the brain of someone with addiction has the opportunity to heal and rebuild the connections that were altered by active addiction.

- Recovery is the process by which a person learns new patterns of living, finds new meaning in life, and moves toward mental, emotional, physical, and spiritual balance.

Recovery is a process of change. This process of change includes learning how to think and act differently. After all, *the only way to get different results is to do things differently.*

For most people, change is difficult and scary. There is a natural fear of the unknown and the uncertainty that goes hand-in-hand with it. It can be hard to do anything that's different or unfamiliar because anything that is unfamiliar tends to be uncomfortable. And the more different or unfamiliar it is, the more uncomfortable it tends to be. It takes strength and courage to do anything that is uncomfortable. That's why doing things differently from the way you've done them in the past always takes strength and courage.

People often stay in situations that are painful and unhealthy (in some cases for many years) because they are familiar with the pain of the specific situation—they know exactly how it works and what the results will be. For many people, it is only when the pain of staying the same outweighs the fear of doing something different that change occurs. Courage is not the absence of fear. Courage is being aware of your fear and doing what you need to do regardless of the fear you may be feeling.

Addiction is a condition that consumes those who struggle with it, increasingly shrinking their world, usurping their freedom, limiting their perspective, and constraining their perceived options. Yet people are much more than their addiction and the pain they seek to avoid. They may suffer with addiction, but can grow beyond it to achieve a value-directed life worth living.

As described in the Introduction, successful, sustained recovery requires two levels of change: awareness and action. Without awareness, the ability to take necessary action is extremely limited. And yet, awareness, though important, is by itself of limited value. Answering the questions in this workbook will help you develop the understanding and skills you will need to translate awareness into action and construct a solid foundation of recovery that you can continue to build on.

The definition of recovery used here mirrors that of the Substance Abuse and Mental Health Services Administration (SAMHSA) of the US Department of Health and Human Services released in 2011 and updated in 2012. SAMHSA's definition captures the most essential, common experiences of the recovery process:

> A process of change through which individuals improve their health and wellness, live a self-directed life, and strive to reach their full potential.

In addition, SAMHSA also offers these Guiding Principles of Recovery (www.samhsa.gov):

- **Recovery emerges from hope.** The belief that recovery is real provides the essential and motivating message of a better future—that people can and do overcome the internal and external challenges, barriers, and obstacles that confront them.

- **Recovery is person-driven.** Self-determination and self-direction are the foundations for recovery as individuals define their own life goals and design their unique path(s) toward those goals.

- **Recovery occurs via many pathways.** Individuals are unique with distinct needs, strengths, preferences, goals, culture, and backgrounds, including trauma experiences that affect and determine their pathway(s) to recovery. Abstinence from the use of alcohol, illicit drugs, and non-prescribed medications is the goal for those with addiction.

- **Recovery is holistic.** Recovery encompasses an individual's whole life, including mind, body, spirit, and community. The array of services and supports available should be integrated and coordinated.

> ...individuals have a personal responsibility for their own self-care and journeys of recovery.

- **Recovery is supported by peers and allies.** Mutual support and mutual aid groups, including the sharing of experiential knowledge and skills, as well as social learning, play an invaluable role in recovery.

- **Recovery is supported through relationships and social networks.** An important factor in the recovery process is the presence and involvement of people who believe in the person's ability to recover; who offer hope, support, and encouragement; and who also suggest strategies and resources for change.

- **Recovery is culturally based and influenced.** Culture and cultural background in all of its diverse representations, including values, traditions, and beliefs, are keys in determining a person's journey and unique pathway to recovery.

- **Recovery is supported by addressing trauma.** The experience of trauma (such as physical or sexual abuse, domestic violence, war, natural disasters, and others) is often a precursor to or associated with alcohol and other drug use, mental health problems, and related issues. Services and support should be trauma-informed to foster safety (physical and emotional) and trust, as well as promote choice, empowerment, and collaboration.

- **Recovery involves individual, family, and community strengths and responsibility.** Individuals, families, and communities have strengths and resources that serve as a foundation for recovery. In addition, individuals have a personal responsibility for their own self-care and journeys of recovery.

- **Recovery is based on respect.** Community, systems, and societal acceptance and appreciation for people affected by mental health and substance use problems—including protecting their rights and eliminating discrimination—are crucial in achieving recovery. There is a need to acknowledge that taking steps toward recovery may require great courage. Self-acceptance, developing a positive and meaningful sense of identity, and regaining belief in one's self are particularly important.

Without abstinence, recovery is not possible. However, recovery is much more than simply remaining abstinent from the specific manifestations of addiction. It involves becoming consciously aware of the thoughts, emotional reactions, and patterns that get in your way, and replacing self-defeating behaviors with healthy, growth-enhancing ways of relating to yourself, to others, and to the world. Recovery is also about following direction and becoming willing to change.

> Recovery consists of two basic parts: 1) getting clean/abstinent—discontinuing using and stopping the vicious circle of active addiction; and 2) staying clean/ abstinent and in recovery—finding pathways to live in an ongoing way without using and learning how to live a whole, healthy, and balanced life. Believe it or not, getting clean is the easy part because it only has to happen once. Staying clean is much harder because it's a continuous, daily process.

The information you learn, the conscious awareness you develop, and the skills you practice will be the keys that unlock the door to successful ongoing recovery. Recovery involves learning and applying solutions to the various challenges that life will present to you. The more solutions you can apply that work for you, the better you will be able to face and address the different problems you may experience. Each and every time you get through a difficult situation, challenge, or problem without using, your recovery gets a little stronger.

STAYING IN RECOVERY: THE FOUR POINTS OF BALANCE

Because addiction has mental, emotional, physical, and spiritual components, recovery requires finding and maintaining mental, emotional, physical, and spiritual balance. Successful, sustained recovery requires balance between these four life domains, as well as within each of them—in other words, being balanced mentally, emotionally, physically, and spiritually.

Balance between and within each of the four points is neither solid nor fixed; it is almost always in motion. You may find it helpful to think of it in terms of a see-saw or teeter-totter, a piece of play equipment once common to school yards and playgrounds. Typically, two children or groups of children sit on opposite ends of a wooden plank balanced in the middle riding up and down so that as one end goes down, the other end goes up in an alternating manner. Sometimes the movement of the see-saw is more extreme, going all the way up and then down, back and forth at high speed; and sometimes, it is slower, more gradual, and softer.

The intense, rapidly fluctuating movement resembles the extreme mental, emotional, physical, and spiritual shifts that characterize active addiction. It can be exhilarating, but there are serious potential threats to health and safety—it's easy to fall off or get hurt. The slower, more gentle back and forth with its milder ups

and downs reflect what people are more likely to experience when they are in a process of recovery, consciously working toward mental, emotional, physical, and spiritual balance.

Although there may be brief moments when the see saw is perfectly balanced, this never lasts long. The vast majority of the time there is some movement as the respective ends of the plank go up and down even slightly and subtly. The same is true of the state of mental, emotional, physical, and spiritual balance, even in recovery and under the best of circumstances. As the circumstances of your life change, so will your state of balance.

From an early age, we are conditioned to categorize experiences, including the experience of emotions and physical sensations, in terms of whether they are "good" or "bad." In this context, sadness, anxiety, fear, guilt, shame, anger, and physical pain are viewed as bad or negative, while happiness, joy, contentment, peace of mind, and being pain-free are interpreted as good or positive. Consequently, it becomes natural to want to avoid experiences judged to be bad, negative, or in other words, painful. When we experience pain—whether the source of that pain is physical, mental, emotional, or spiritual—we generally attempt to escape from it. After all, who wants to be in pain?

People challenged by addiction seek to avoid distressing emotions and physical pain through the use of substances and/or activities like gambling, eating, or sex. The acute effects of using may keep the painful feelings and physical sensations away for a time, after which they return, typically with increased intensity and commonly accompanied by newly created problems. Such strategies to escape emotional and physical pain only make it worse, and in the process deepen the experience of suffering.

Suffering is a function of the beliefs people attach to their emotional and physical pain. For instance, whenever the belief exists that someone shouldn't be in pain and in turn, it is something to be avoided at all costs, that person will experience suffering. Ironically, the harder someone works to avoid the experience of pain, the greater his or her suffering tends to be. Increased suffering, that acute feeling of being in distress, further escalates the need for relief through using, and the vicious circle of active addiction progressively intensifies.

> The acute effects of using may keep the painful feelings and physical sensations away for a time, after which they return, typically with increased intensity and commonly accompanied by newly created problems.

The greater someone's suffering, the more out of balance mentally, emotionally, physically, and spiritually he or she tends to be. The following are experiences that contribute to imbalance in your life. Check all that apply to you and add any that are not included.

MENTAL IMBALANCE

_____ Negative thoughts in general

_____ Thinking negatively about yourself

_____ Thinking you are a victim

_____ Believing you have no control of your life

_____ Thinking issues are worse than they are

_____ Thinking issues will never get better

_____ Other: _____

_____ Other: _____

Identify which of the above forms of mental imbalance you struggle with most and describe how it affects you.

_____

_____

_____

EMOTIONAL IMBALANCE

_____ Depression

_____ Guilt and shame

_____ Anger and resentment

_____ Unresolved childhood issues

_____ Anxiety

_____ Feeling trapped

_____ Poor self-image

_____ Other: _____

_____ Other: _____

Identify which of the above forms of emotional imbalance you struggle with most and describe how it affects you.

_____

_____

_____

PHYSICAL IMBALANCE

_____ Lack of exercise

_____ Poor eating habits

_____ Loss of physical abilities

_____ Loss of functioning

_____ Insomnia or sleeping too much

_____ Sexual problems

_____ Inability to work and support yourself and your family

_____ Other: _____

_____ Other: _____

Identify which of the above forms of physical imbalance you struggle with most and describe how it affects you.

_____

_____

_____

SPIRITUAL IMBALANCE

_____ No sense of purpose in life

_____ Lack of trust

_____ Lack of faith

_____ Feelings of isolation

_____ Alienation from God/Spirit/Higher Power

_____ Other: _____

_____ Other: _____

Identify which of the above forms of spiritual imbalance you struggle with most and describe how it affects you.

_____

_____

_____

MENTAL BALANCE

With mental balance, you observe and pay attention to your thinking. Balanced thinking results in realistic expectations and the ability to focus energy and effort in making progress toward specific goals. Common characteristics of a balanced mental experience include: keeping a positive attitude; observing, accepting, and challenging your thoughts; setting achievable goals; being open-minded and willing to try new approaches; and having realistic hope.

Describe two steps you can take to begin the process of moving toward better mental balance.

1. _____

_____

_____

2. _____

_____

_____

EMOTIONAL BALANCE

With emotional balance, you accept your emotions and know it's okay to feel whatever you are feeling. You are more independent from the opinions and beliefs of others and pay closer attention to your inner voice. Common characteristics of a balanced emotional experience include: understanding feelings are neither good nor bad (not judging feelings); observing and learning to tolerate uncomfortable, painful feelings; and seeing that simply experiencing emotions will not hurt you; in fact, not feeling emotions makes you hurt worse; knowing that allowing yourself to feel your emotions results in healing, while avoidance results in ongoing suffering; and understanding that balanced thoughts contribute to balanced emotions.

Describe two steps you can take to begin the process of moving toward better emotional balance.

1. _____

_____

_____

2. _____

_____

_____

PHYSICAL BALANCE

Physical balance requires you to be mindful and respectful of your body, which includes paying attention to the messages it sends to your brain. You evaluate the state of your body, without becoming preoccupied. Common characteristics of physical balance include: being aware of your physical status, and what you need to take care of yourself physically; eating nutritious foods; avoiding toxins; exercising regularly; getting enough sleep; and practicing relaxation.

Describe two steps you can take to begin the process of moving toward better physical balance.

1. _____

_____

_____

2. _____

_____

_____

SPIRITUAL BALANCE

With spiritual balance, whatever life brings, you are able to cope with it and know you are okay. You are able to find meaning and purpose even in situations that are painful. You live in and accept each day as it comes and put effort into changing yourself instead of trying to change others.

Common characteristics of a balanced spiritual experience include: having a sense of connection to something beyond yourself; accepting who you are and your place in the world; having a sense of purpose and meaning; being open to challenging your beliefs; having values, standards, and ethics that you embrace; and having increased awareness of a connection with self, others, Higher Power/ God/Universe/Spirit/Divine, through some sort of regular spiritual practice.

Describe two steps you can take to begin the process of moving toward better spiritual balance.

1. _____

_____

_____

2. _____

_____

_____

Balance, like recovery from addiction, is a journey. Life's circumstances and events create challenges along the way. As opposed to viewing these challenges as obstacles, you are invited to see them as opportunities for learning and growing and healing. This journey is an ongoing process; it does not have an end point.

Striving for perfect balance, while an understandable goal, is simply not realistic. After all, life is rarely perfect. Every once in a while you may be blessed with brief experiences of what seems to you like perfection, but these moments are fleeting. In fact, focusing on achieving perfection can actually contribute to imbalance because it creates unnecessary stress and unrealistic expectations.

As you become aware of circumstances in your life that are out of balance, it is helpful to resist the urge to overcorrect through extreme or impulsive actions. There are no quick fixes. Changes are most healthy and effective when made gradually yet progressively, taking into consideration all four points of balance: mental, emotional, physical, and spiritual. There may be times when it is useful to concentrate more on one or two of these four points than the others. However, all four points represent the most essential aspects of being human and are all connected to each other. It is not helpful or healthy to address them individually without consideration of the others. When all four points are working together in balance, they produce a powerful healing effect wherein the whole is much greater than the sum of its parts. A more in-depth discussion is provided in Pathways to Recovery.

One solution to restore balance in your thoughts, emotions, and behavior is to consciously separate what you may want from the reality of the situation. It's normal, natural, and understandable to want life's details to be the way you want them, but recovery requires an ability to accept the things you cannot change.

THE SERENITY PRAYER

Applying the Serenity Prayer and focusing consciously on identifying the things you cannot change, as well as what you can do to better accept them will make noticeable, positive, and healthy differences in your life. It is essential to remember one factor you can always change is how you respond to the people, events, and situations in your life. "People, places, and things" will not change for you. In some cases, you will need to change your reaction to them. In others, you need to simply accept them and move on to the best of your ability. Using the Serenity Prayer as a tool to clarify the things you cannot change, and therefore need to find a way to accept versus the things you can change, is a solution-oriented approach to achieving balance and strengthening your recovery.

> "Grant me the serenity to accept the things I cannot change, the courage to change the things I can, and the wisdom to know the difference."

Related to your addiction, identify something you cannot change and need to accept.

_____

_____

Describe how you will begin to go about accepting it.

_____

_____

_____

Related to your addiction, identify something you can change.

_____

_____

Describe how you will begin to go about changing it.

_____

_____

_____

Describe how you can tell the difference between what you can and cannot change.

_____

_____

_____

The process of changing your mental, emotional, physical, and spiritual patterns of living requires patience and persistence because it doesn't happen easily or quickly; but it does come with the new skills you'll learn in your recovery practices. Strive to take your recovery a day at a time, incorporating the Serenity Prayer throughout the day as you make an effort to achieve balance within each of the four points described.

> It is important to be aware that you are not responsible for becoming addicted, but you are responsible for maintaining your recovery!

NOTES

_____

_____

_____

_____

_____

_____

_____

_____

_____

_____

ROADBLOCKS TO RECOVERY

Potential Challenges and Obstacles That Can Interfere with Your Recovery

There are many potential challenges along the path of recovery. Some of these challenges are so common that nearly everyone who enters recovery from addiction encounters them. As a result, maintaining abstinence and building your recovery will require you to be able to recognize and deal with them successfully. These challenges can present roadblocks that obstruct your way or potholes that you can fall into. They may get in your way temporarily or for a long time, depending on how clearly you see them, how prepared you are for them, and how you respond to them. The rest of this section will help you identify and prepare for many of the challenges you can expect to encounter along your path of recovery.

Keep in mind the focus of this section is on the potential roadblocks that can interfere with your recovery process. The solutions and strategies that can provide pathways to strengthen your recovery will be covered in the next section Pathways to Recovery.

Detoxing after Detox: Post-Acute Withdrawal Syndrome (PAWS)

Most people, including those with addiction, their friends and loved ones, and even some medical professionals and therapists, seem to believe that "normal" functioning—physical, mental, emotional, and spiritual—should return as soon as the substances are out of the body (on completion of detoxification—also known as acute withdrawal) or the addictive activities/behaviors are stopped. As nice as this might sound, it is simply not true.

> Post-acute withdrawal
> is an uncomfortable,
> but necessary process
> that everyone in
> early recovery must
> go through…

Active addiction dramatically changes brain structure and functioning in the areas that govern thinking, feeling, and behaving; these changes include eating and sleeping habits. Depending on the length and intensity of active addiction—that is, how much and for how long an individual has used substances and/or engaged in addictive activities, the withdrawal process can actually continue for weeks or months after he or she has stopped using. This is known as **Post-Acute** (sometimes called **protracted**) **Withdrawal Syndrome** or simply post-acute withdrawal.

Post-acute withdrawal is an uncomfortable, but necessary process that everyone in early recovery must go through, as the brain and body are healing and being rewired to adjust to living without the substances/activities of active addiction. Post-acute withdrawal can cause difficulties in thinking, concentration, attention span, judgment, memory, sleep, appetite, and mood such as irritability, anxiety, and depression. It is not unusual for those in early recovery to experience challenges in these areas for weeks or even months.

Describe how post-acute withdrawal seems to be affecting you physically, including eating and sleeping habits.

_____

_____

_____

_____

Describe how post-acute withdrawal may be affecting your thinking, including your ability to concentrate and pay attention.

_____

_____

_____

_____

Describe how post-acute withdrawal may be affecting you emotionally, including the degree to which you find yourself irritable, angry, anxious, and/or depressed.

_____

_____

_____

_____

The discomfort of post-acute withdrawal is often a driving factor for people who relapse during early recovery. Many

1. Can't stand it.

2. Don't want to deal with it.

3. Believe that if being in recovery is *this* uncomfortable, they might as well use.

This thought process is normal for those in early recovery. But as uncomfortable as it can feel, it is extremely important to be aware that post-acute withdrawal is temporary. Even if it takes several months to pass, it always does.

Describe how post-acute withdrawal can be a potential roadblock to your recovery (be specific).

_____

_____

_____

_____

Playing Defense: Denial, Minimizing, Rationalizing, and Avoidance

The disease of addiction is both treacherous and seductive in the ways it attempts to convince you that you don't have it.

Defense mechanisms—we'll call them **defenses**—are unconscious psychological processes that occur outside of your conscious awareness to help you cope with painful aspects of reality. It is part of human nature to avoid painful truths. Defenses help make this happen. They serve the purpose of self-protection by protecting you mentally and emotionally from too much anxiety, fear, stress, or pain. Everyone who struggles with addiction is in significant emotional (and sometimes physical) pain.

Defense mechanisms provide shelter from the storm of distressing situations with which you cannot currently cope. The use of defense mechanisms is normal and natural, and everyone uses them throughout life. However, defense mechanisms become problematic and unhealthy when using them enables destructive or self-defeating behaviors, such as addiction, to continue. When this happens, defenses become overused and work too well, overprotecting people to the point they become disconnected from reality.

In active addiction, denial, minimizing, rationalizing, and avoidance are the most commonly used defenses. People in active addiction rely on these defenses to protect themselves from the mental and emotional pain that is related to their using. They provide fuel for continuing to use substances and/or activities, even as the negative consequences of active addiction continue to grow. These defenses keep those struggling with addiction from being able to accurately see and admit many of the problems that are painfully obvious to others.

> The use of defense mechanisms is normal and natural,
> and everyone uses them throughout life.

DENIAL

Denial regularly walks hand-in-hand with addiction. People in denial seem to ignore unpleasant facts and reject information that contradicts what they need to believe. For those with the disease of addiction, denial most often involves refusing to admit they have a problem because it would create too much anxiety, stress, or pain.

Thinking or believing addiction "won't happen to me" is another form of denial. Denial can also take other forms. You may think, *I might have a problem with heroin but I've never had a problem with alcohol so I can drink*, or *I have a problem with crack (or meth) but I've never had a problem with pain pills and since the doctor prescribed Vicodin for my sprained ankle, I can take them. Smoking pot is no big deal; I can do that. Besides, it's now legal in some states.*

Even if you accept that you have the disease of addiction and begin a process of recovery, denial can reemerge. After a period of abstinence and with some time in recovery, denial may come back and try to convince you that you no longer have a problem. And since you no longer have a problem, you may think you can use a little of this or a little of that.

Denial enables you to believe you can control your using and that you do not have the disease of addiction no matter how much evidence to the contrary exists. Even when everyone close to you can see your addiction clearly, denial can keep you convinced your biggest problem is that these people won't leave you alone and that if everyone would stop nagging you, your life would be fine.

> Denial enables you to believe you can control your using and that you do not have the disease of addiction no matter how much evidence to the contrary exists.

 Describe two examples of denial in your active addiction.

1. _____

_____

_____

2. _____

_____

_____

Denial is sometimes confused with dishonesty. It is important to be aware that the unconscious process of denial (being unable to accept and admit the truth because it's so painful) is different from dishonesty or lying (when you are consciously aware of what the truth is and choose to make statements that you know are false or misleading).

Even when you can mobilize the strength and courage to admit your using is beyond your ability to control it, denial can keep you from accepting the fact that you need help in order to recover. Denial tries to convince you that you can do it alone. But realistically, if you could recover by yourself, without the help of others, you already would have. How many times did you attempt to do it all by yourself? How many times did it not work? Your denial may even be talking to you right now, whispering in your ear, still trying to con you into believing this is all a bunch of baloney and that you actually don't need any help at all.

If denial were to reemerge during your recovery, what form(s) might it take? What would it look like?

_____

_____

_____

Describe how denial can get in the way of your recovery (be specific).

_____

_____

_____

MINIMIZING

Minimizing is sort of a minor league version of denial. Instead of denying the existence of something painful, minimizing is a way of making it seem better than it is—to others and to oneself.

For example you might say, "I only had two beers today," when in fact you drank a six pack, or "I only smoked pot," when you also took pain pills, or "I only gamble a couple of times a month," when the reality is you gamble three times per week.

> Those with addiction often minimize
>
> How much they use.
> How often they use.
> What substances or activities they use.
>
> The negative consequences of using on various areas of their lives, such as relationships, finances, and health.

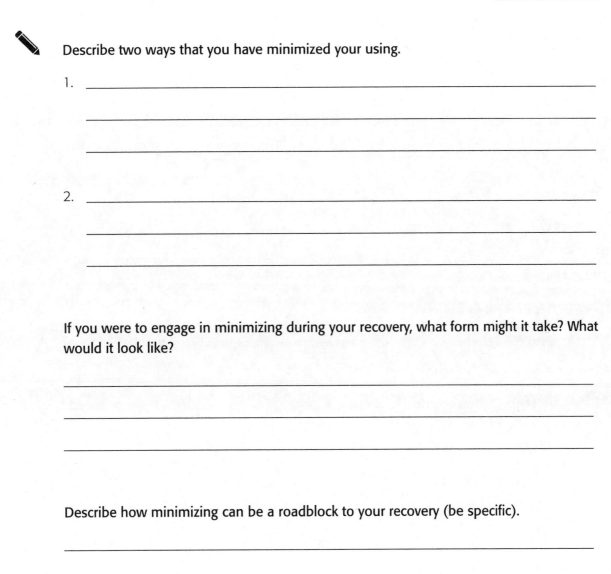

Describe two ways that you have minimized your using.

1. _____

_____

_____

2. _____

_____

_____

If you were to engage in minimizing during your recovery, what form might it take? What would it look like?

_____

_____

_____

Describe how minimizing can be a roadblock to your recovery (be specific).

_____

_____

_____

RATIONALIZING

Rationalizing—sometimes referred to as **justifying**—is an attempt to explain behaviors, feelings, thoughts, or desires, which create anxiety, fear, stress, or pain to make them seem more appropriate or acceptable. Rationalizing serves to deflect responsibility away from you. It is not about *what* happened so much as it relates to *why* it (whatever "it" might be) happened. Rationalizing is a way of trying to make one's motives seem more acceptable or reasonable to oneself or to others.

For example, people with addiction may admit to using daily, but think it's okay and/or they are not responsible for it because:

1. His or her partner is nagging them.

2. He or she is in pain: "I know my prescription is for four pills a day, but I was in a huge amount of pain so I took seven."

3. He or she is under loads of stress.

4. He or she has been good lately or has been working especially hard, and so "deserves it."

Describe two examples of how you rationalized certain incidents that happened in your active addiction.

1. _____

_____

_____

2. _____

_____

_____

If you were to engage in rationalizing during your recovery, what form might it take? What would it look like?

_____

_____

_____

Describe how rationalizing can be a roadblock to your recovery (be specific).

_____

_____

_____

AVOIDANCE

Avoidance is staying away from situations, people, or activities because they create anxiety, stress, or pain. It is about keeping distance from uncomfortable situations. The discomfort, for example, may come from not wanting to face the natural negative consequences of continued use.

Avoidance may include removing oneself physically from a situation, such as not going home to face an angry partner or to work to face the boss. It may also involve finding ways not to talk about or even think about the serious problems addiction has created in one's life.

Describe two ways that you have tried to avoid the negative consequences of your addiction.

1. _____

_____

_____

2. _____

_____

_____

If you were to engage in avoidance during your recovery, what form might it take? What would it look like?

_____

_____

_____

Describe how avoidance can be a roadblock to your recovery (be specific).

_____

_____

_____

> The brain adapts to repetitive experiences (doing the same things over and over) by forming memory connections or tracks of which we are not consciously aware.

Substituting One Manifestation of Addiction for Another

The brain adapts to repetitive experiences (doing the same things over and over) by forming memory connections or tracks of which we are not consciously aware. These unconscious memory tracks are the foundation of the "habits" of addiction. Such habits can be so difficult to control because they are created by changes in brain functioning and are outside of conscious awareness. The intense desire that those with addiction experience for their drug or activity—weeks, months, and sometimes even years after they last used—is one example of the strength of these memory tracks.

These tracks, along with the core characteristics and active dynamics of addiction, dramatically increase the potential for the disease of addiction to manifest in other forms that have not previously presented problems. Once addiction has taken hold in your life in any form, it becomes much more likely to emerge or, after a period of abstinence, reemerge in another form.

As long as the following core characteristics go unaddressed you will continue to be vulnerable to addiction in all of its manifestations.

- Internal emptiness

- Having a sense of or seeing yourself as "different" or as "not fitting in"

- An inability to tolerate uncomfortable or painful feelings

At that point, the active dynamics of obsessive thinking, compulsive behaving, self-centered attitudes, and the discomfort of withdrawal push the spark along the fuse toward the dynamite.

Whether it happens sooner or later, it's only a matter of time until things once again blow up in the predictable results of:

- Progression, as addiction in its new and different manifestation increases in intensity, frequency, and severity.

- Loss of control as your ability to limit the amount and frequency of use slips further and further away.

- Continued use despite increasingly serious negative consequences.

There is a well-known saying that "nature abhors a vacuum." When there is empty space, it will always get filled with something. Addiction is an attempt to fill an internal hole or emptiness with external things—whether substances, activities, or other people. If this internal emptiness is not filled with matters that are positive, healthy, and recovery-supportive, it will inevitably be filled with other factors, usually unhealthy ones that you are familiar with, because anything that is familiar is naturally more comfortable than something that is less familiar. As a result, what is familiar to you has a powerful, natural, and understandable pull, almost like that of a magnet.

If you are reading this, you have significant experience with filling your own internal emptiness with substances, and perhaps activities as well. The pull for you to return to these familiar ways of filling any internal holes you experience or to substitute other unhealthy ways may be strong.

> Addiction is an attempt to fill an internal hole or emptiness with external things—whether substances, activities, or other people.

 Please review the following list of substances. Place an "R" next to those you've used most recently and a "P" next to those you have used in the past.

_____ Heroin/opiates	_____ Prescription pain meds	_____ Cocaine/crack
_____ Methamphetamine	_____ Alcohol	_____ Marijuana
_____ Inhalants	_____ Sedatives (sleeping meds)	_____ Hallucinogens

_____ Tranquilizers (Xanax, Valium, Klonopin)

Others (please list) _____

_____

When you have become addicted to any substance, crack cocaine for example, you are at extremely high risk for your addiction to manifest in the use of other drugs, whether it might be alcohol, prescription pain medications, pot, etc.

Describe two ways you have thought about or engaged in substituting one manifestation of addiction for another, using substances.

1. _____

_____

_____

2. _____

_____

_____

If you were to engage in substituting one manifestation of addiction for another, using substance, what form(s) might it take?

_____

_____

_____

When experienced in moderation (in a balanced way), most of the activities and experiences listed below are simply part of life and can be healthy, up to a point. However, people, especially those who struggle with the disease of addiction, can get caught up in them in ways that are obsessive, compulsive, self-centered, and problematic.

They all have the potential to be used excessively and as temporary external "fixes" for the internal emptiness that addiction attempts to fill. In other words, people may try to "fix" by using these activities to change the way they feel—to feel better or to feel different.

Place a "C" next to those you use currently; an "R" next to those you used until recently; and a "P" next to those you have used as a fix in the past.

_____ Gambling	_____ Sex	_____ Shopping
_____ Pornography	_____ Food/eating	_____ Love/relationships
_____ Internet use	_____ Video gaming	_____ Fantasy sports
_____ Making money	_____ Spending money	_____ Work
_____ Television	_____ Exercise	_____ Cutting/self-harming
_____ Tattooing	_____ Thrill-seeking	_____ Watching sports

Others (please list) _____

_____

Arguably, the most insidious and potentially dangerous manifestations of addiction are those with social acceptability and adaptive qualities, for example, work. After all, work, even to excess, is not only socially acceptable it is often highly valued. And who could possibly find fault in an activity that can help one's self and one's family do better financially? However, an excessive relationship with anything, no matter how socially acceptable, can have increasingly negative consequences. When the core characteristics, facilitating factors, active dynamics, and predictable outcomes of addiction as described earlier are present, so is the disease of addiction.

> …an excessive relationship with anything, no matter how socially acceptable, can have increasingly negative consequences.

Describe two ways you have thought about or engaged in substituting one manifestation of addiction for another, using activities.

1. _____

_____

_____

2. _____

_____

_____

If you were to engage in substituting one manifestation of addiction for another, using activities now, what form(s) would it most likely take?

_____

_____

_____

> Relapse is not merely the act of using; it is a process that starts well before the actual use of one or more of the manifestations of addiction…

Because addiction is addiction, once you are addicted to any drug, including alcohol, even when you are in recovery, you are automatically at a much greater risk of your addiction also manifesting in an activity, such as gambling, eating, sex, shopping/spending, Internet use, and video gaming. The process of active addiction alters brain structure and functioning in ways that turn the road to seeking pleasure and avoiding discomfort into an interstate freeway for many different types of vehicles traveling at high speeds.

The defenses of denial, minimizing, and rationalizing all contribute to the internal process that leads to substituting one manifestation of addiction for another. This process can progress slowly and so subtly that you have no conscious awareness of it. Relapse is not merely the act of using; it is a process that starts well before the actual use of one or more of the manifestations of addiction—often with a gradual return to the same kinds of thinking, ways of coping (or not coping) with thoughts, feelings, and behaviors you demonstrated during your active addiction.

As mentioned before, substituting one manifestation of addiction for another is much like switching where you are sitting on a boat that is sinking—you may be able to stay dry for a little longer, but you will still end up in the water, with all of the potential dangers that go with it.

If you were to use denial, minimizing, or rationalizing to engage in substituting one manifestation of addiction for another, what form might it take? What do you think it would look like?

_____

_____

_____

Describe how substituting one manifestation of addiction for another can be a potential roadblock to your recovery (be specific).

_____

_____

_____

Acting Out on Anger and Resentments

People with addiction frequently experience problems related to anger and resentment. Anger and resentment are closely connected. Without anger, resentment cannot form. Anger that is expressed in unhealthy ways and the resentment it fuels are serious roadblocks to recovery.

> Anger is a strong feeling of displeasure and upset aroused by some sort of wrong or injustice, either real or imagined, in the present.

Over time, the person, place, thing, or event that caused the original anger and led to resentment may even be forgotten, while the resentment remains like still-smoldering embers left after the flames of a fire die down. The fire no longer rages, but the embers remain hot and at risk of causing more fires. As long as these embers continue to burn, they create negative distractions that take time, attention, and energy away from recovery.

ANGER

Anger is a strong feeling of displeasure and upset aroused by some sort of wrong or injustice, either real or imagined, in the present. It is a normal, natural emotion that everyone has encountered and experienced at various points in life. For some people, anger is an almost automatic emotional reaction when daily events don't go the way they want them to go. Addicts, in particular, often become angry when they cannot get whatever it is they want when they want it.

Describe the kinds of situations in which you usually become angry (be specific).

_____

_____

_____

_____

How do you usually react when you feel angry?

_____

_____

_____

_____

When you get angry, what does it look like? If you were watching yourself reacting in anger on a video screen, what would you see?

_____

_____

_____

_____

In most circumstances, anger is actually a secondary emotion.

It is important to be aware that in many situations, anger is a healthy and appropriate emotional reaction. Problems with anger usually occur in how this powerful feeling is expressed. Anger can be expressed along a continuum—from suppressing it (i.e., not expressing it outwardly, keeping it inside to the point where a person may not even be aware that he or she is angry), all the way to uncontrolled rage, which can include screaming, verbal abuse, property damage, and even physical violence.

In most circumstances, anger is actually a secondary emotion. It often forms immediately and automatically—happening unconsciously so there may be no conscious awareness of it—in response to something (or someone) that brings up feelings of hurt, fear, and/or inadequacy. When most people experience these primary emotions, they feel vulnerable and their energy and attention are focused internally. This inward focus on one's own vulnerabilities tends to be extremely uncomfortable.

Describe a recent instance when you became angry. Identify where you were, who you were with, and what happened.

_____

_____

_____

_____

Identify the underlying primary emotions your anger may have kept hidden in the above situation.

_____

_____

_____

Anger serves several defensive purposes for people struggling with addiction. It deflects uncomfortable primary emotions so they can be avoided or kept at a distance; it provides a sense of power and control; and it directs focus outward to identifiable, external scapegoats. After all, it is almost always easier and more comfortable to focus on the actions of others than it is to focus on oneself.

Identify and describe the purposes that using anger to keep these underlying emotions under cover serves for you. What do you get from covering them up with your anger?

_____

_____

_____

Identify and describe two ways of dealing with feelings of anger that can get in the way of your recovery (be specific).

1. _____

_____

_____

2. _____

_____

_____

> While anger is about experiences that happen in the present, resentments focus on what happened in the past.

RESENTMENTS

People with addiction often have resentments. **Resentments** are negative feelings, basically ill will and upset toward some*one* or some*thing* in the past experienced as wrong, unjust, insulting, or disrespectful. Resentments are created when people get angry with a person, institution, or situation and hold on to that anger, refusing to let go of it. "It's (whatever "it" is) their fault; they are to blame!" are common reactions.

While anger is about experiences that happen in the present, resentments focus on what happened in the past. They are a re-experiencing of past events and the old feelings of anger connected to them. The continuous mental and emotional reenactment of past events that occurs with resentments is similar to replaying a movie with yourself in the starring role as the victim—the DVD plays over and over in your head reinforcing your thoughts and feelings connected to the past injustice. The perception of being wronged creates a victim mentality. This makes recovery more difficult because such a mentality interferes with the ability to take responsibility for one's own choices and actions.

Identify the resentments you are currently holding on to.

_____

_____

_____

_____

Describe the unhealthy, negative effects of holding on to these resentments.

_____

_____

_____

_____

It is sometimes a surprise for people in early recovery to learn they can have resentments toward themselves for perceived mistakes, failures, or wrongs done to others. There are many reasons people use to justify their anger and resentments.

So-called "justified" resentments can be especially difficult to address because the person holding the resentment is convinced that he or she is right and the other party is wrong. Carrying resentments, even when they could potentially be justified, always interferes with the recovery process.

Describe the biggest resentments you have toward yourself.

_____

_____

_____

_____

There is a saying that states, "When you resent somebody, you become that person's slave." The stronger the resentment is, the more time you spend thinking about it and getting caught up in the anger connected to it. This is a form of mental, emotional, and spiritual slavery. As it has been described, holding on to a resentment is like drinking poison and expecting the other person/place/thing to die; ultimately, the person holding the resentment is the one who suffers most.

Identify at least two ways of handling resentments that can get in the way of your recovery (be specific).

1. _____

_____

_____

2. _____

_____

_____

Those with addiction often carry their anger and resentments wherever they go. Like an unnecessary suitcase, it is baggage that weighs them down and requires attention and energy. As long as you are focused on the people and situations you are angry with and resentful toward, you are not focusing on your recovery and what you need to do to abstain from addictive behaviors.

Escaping and Numbing Uncomfortable, Painful Feelings

As noted earlier, substances and activities like gambling, eating, and sex are mood altering. One of the desired effects of using drugs and/or activities is that they provide a way for people to change the way they feel. Through the use of substances or engaging in certain activities, people seek to feel "good" or feel "better." People typically begin using drugs or choose activities because they can temporarily avoid or lessen feelings of emotional or physical discomfort, such as anxiety, depression, physical pain, fear, boredom, and/or stress. Remember, *using* includes both the use of substances and involvement in activities that are connected to addiction. Drugs and activities provide a way to escape from or "turn down the volume" on these uncomfortable, painful feelings.

Early recovery is often an emotional roller coaster that swings from exhilarating highs to painful lows. In recovery, you start to feel emotions that using helped to keep at a distance. You may begin to experience more fully, feelings that you have struggled with since even before you started to use.

> Remember, *using* includes both the use of substances and involvement in activities that are connected to addiction.

One of the core characteristics that make people vulnerable to addiction is an inability to tolerate uncomfortable, painful feelings. Compared to most other people, those with addiction tend to be especially emotionally sensitive. They frequently experience emotional pain more deeply and more often than others do. The distress such discomfort creates can emerge quickly and without warning. It can feel overwhelming and as though it will last forever.

One of the most challenging roadblocks to recovery is working through the discomfort to allow yourself to feel, accept, and co-exist with the distressing and often painful emotions of fear, anxiety, sadness, depression, grief, guilt, shame, and loneliness.

FEAR

Fear is the feeling of being frightened or scared. The emotion of fear focuses on the future—it's about what you are afraid could happen or might possibly happen or will happen. All forms of fear stem from "fear of the unknown" and "fear of change." In twelve-step recovery programs, the word FEAR is sometimes used as an acronym—"**F**orget **E**verything **A**nd **R**un"—to describe how people with addiction often act on feelings of fear.

Fear is a natural human emotion necessary for survival. It helps us respond effectively to threatening situations. Walking out into the middle of a busy highway should cause fear. If someone points a gun at you and threatens to shoot you, obviously fear is a healthy reaction to the situation. Irrational fear is fear that lacks reason and clarity, like a cloud that envelops you. Paralyzing fear keeps people frozen in place, unable to move forward.

> The emotion of fear focuses on the future…

Fear becomes problematic when you allow it to paralyze you by keeping you from doing what you need to do to function in the world. Using can sometimes mask fear, making it easier to pretend it's not there. It's not unusual for people to act more brave or fearless than they otherwise would when they are under the influence.

People often fear

- losing what they have: people/relationships, possessions, power, money, jobs, health, or prestige;

- getting hurt;

- not getting what they want, especially when they want it desperately;

- the discomfort of post-acute withdrawal will never end;

- life without using will be boring;

- they can't live without using;

- when they are in physical or emotional pain, it will last forever;

- they won't be successful in recovery (so why even bother trying?); and

- that they will never be able to overcome the negative consequences of their using on finances, family, health, and employment.

Fear can also feed on itself, becoming a vicious circle where the more fearful you are, the more fearful you become, and the less able to function you are likely to be.

Identify and describe your two greatest fears related to your addiction (be specific).

1. _____

_____

_____

2. _____

_____

_____

> Fear can be extremely difficult to acknowledge to yourself and others.

Fear can be extremely difficult to acknowledge to yourself and others. Few people like to admit or talk about being scared. In some circles (families, neighborhoods, or other groups of people), feeling scared and expressing fear is viewed as "weakness," making it even harder to discuss with others in the interests of avoiding negative perceptions and judgments.

In this way, you may actually fear talking about being fearful with others.

Fear is one of the main reasons people continue to use and never find recovery. It is also one of the reasons people in recovery relapse.

Even though recovery from active addiction is an incredibly positive and healthy change, it is a huge change in one's life and lifestyle. And as described, fear of change and fear of the unknown and the uncertainty that goes hand-in-hand with it is natural and incredibly powerful.

Identify and describe your two greatest fears related to recovery.

1. _____

_____

_____

2. _____

_____

_____

Describe specifically what it is about each of the above that creates fear for you.

_____

_____

_____

_____

_____

_____

Describe how the way(s) you handle feelings of fear can be a potential roadblock to your recovery.

_____

_____

_____

_____

People sometimes stay in situations that are painful and that they know are unhealthy or even dangerous because they are familiar with the pain of the specific situation. They know it so well that they know exactly how it works and what the results will be. It is the uncertainty and unknowns of making changes and entering unfamiliar territory that they fear. For many people, it is only when the pain of staying the same outweighs the fear of doing something different that change occurs.

ANXIETY

Anxiety is related to fear. In fact, anxiety is basically low-level fear. It can be defined as distressing uneasiness, nervousness, or worry. It is experienced in response to situations anticipated to be threatening. Anxiety is usually accompanied by self-doubt about your capacity to cope with a given situation—whatever the situation may be. The symptoms of anxiety range from sweaty palms and increased heart rate, to increased muscle tension, to breaking out in cold sweats, to an inability to sit still and a feeling of being uncomfortable in your own skin.

A large percentage of those with addiction also struggle with anxiety. It is a roadblock that represents a serious threat to ongoing recovery. Similar to fear, anxiety can be an effect, as well as a contributing factor in using. Sometimes people use to help them feel less anxious. However, after the high wears off and because of how using changes brain chemistry—anxiety is also made worse by using. People experience increased anxiety when

- they are "coming down" and experiencing withdrawal;

- they are worried about where their next "fix" will come from—how they will get the ways and means to continue to use—whether it's the next hit, bottle, bag, hand of cards, pull of a slot machine, orgasm, relationship, spending spree, etc.; or

- they are worried about negative consequences of their using on finances, family, health, and employment.

Identify the issues that bring about the most anxiety for you.

_____

_____

_____

_____

Describe the connection between your using and feelings of anxiety.

_____

_____

_____

_____

Describe how the way(s) you handle feelings of anxiety can be a potential roadblock to your recovery.

_____

_____

_____

DEPRESSION, SADNESS, GRIEF, AND LOSS

The feeling states of sadness, grief, and loss are closely related to one another and often fall underneath the umbrella of depression. **Sadness** refers to a feeling of unhappiness, while **grief** consists of distress related to the process of mourning a loss of some sort.

Depression can be a feeling but also a more enduring emotional condition that exists on a continuum from mild to severe. It is a diagnosable disorder marked by a variety of symptoms. The symptoms of depression can include:

- feelings of sadness
- increased or decreased appetite
- loss of interest and enthusiasm
- decreased self-esteem
- poor concentration or indecision

- difficulty sleeping or sleeping too much
- weight loss or gain
- feelings of helplessness, hopelessness, and/or worthlessness
- fatigue or loss of energy
- thoughts of death or suicidal thoughts

Identify any symptoms of depression you have experienced.

_____

_____

_____

_____

Like anxiety, depression can contribute to using, as well as become a result of using. Sometimes people use to help feel less depressed, but because of how using changes brain chemistry, depression is also made worse by using. Using depletes your brain of some of the chemical messengers—neurotransmitters, most importantly dopamine—that help you to maintain a "normal" mood.

People also commonly feel depressed when they are experiencing withdrawal and when they have to face the problems their using has created or made worse. It may be helpful to know that depression is sometimes thought of as anger turned inwardly against oneself.

Describe the connection between your using and feelings or symptoms of depression.

_____

_____

_____

_____

Describe how depression can be a potential roadblock to your recovery.

_____

_____

_____

Unresolved grief is also often both a contributing cause and a result of using. Grief is a natural emotional state attached to loss. Grieving refers to mourning a loss, a process that can take weeks to months or longer. Loss occurs when someone or something is no longer available to us due to death, injury/illness or other health reasons, the end of a relationship, etc. The more emotionally important the loss, the greater the grief associated with it—and the longer the process of mourning that loss will take.

As addiction progressively gets worse, people begin to suffer more and more losses, such as relationships with family or friends, jobs, financial resources, material possessions, reputation, prestige, health, the ability to work and physically function as before, the ability to participate in previously enjoyed recreational and family activities, self-esteem, and hopes and dreams for the future.

In recovery, an inevitable, yet often under-recognized and under-appreciated loss is that of using. After all, substances and activities may have come to seem like your best friend, lover, and confidante.

In recovery, an inevitable, yet often under-recognized and under-appreciated loss is that of using. After all, substances and activities may have come to seem like your best friend, lover, and confidante. Sometimes, the lifestyle that is associated with using, along with the identity that people have developed in connection with it, is also a surprisingly significant and under-appreciated loss.

Describe your relationship to the specific manifestations of your active addiction.

_____

_____

_____

_____

Describe how the loss of using and the lifestyle connected with using can be a potential roadblock to your recovery.

_____

_____

_____

_____

Describe how unresolved grief related to other losses you've experienced can be a potential roadblock to your recovery.

_____

_____

_____

SHAME AND GUILT

> Guilt and shame often exist in partnership for people with addiction.

Guilt and shame often exist in partnership for people with addiction. **Guilt** is an emotion wherein you feel that you've made a mistake. It is defined as a feeling of having committed some wrong or failed in an obligation. **Shame**, on the other hand, is an emotion where the feeling is that you are a mistake. Shame is defined as a feeling of humiliation or distress that may be attached to "wrong" or foolish behavior. However, often it is not even connected to a specific behavior but to how we perceive ourselves.

The emotional experience of shame is based on a belief that there's something intrinsically wrong with you as a person. Deep inside, you feel fundamentally flawed, and believe that everyone knows it. Being an addict simply feeds into and strengthens this fundamental belief that there is something wrong with you. For many people, it is difficult to escape from the burden of shame that has been internalized as a result of growing up in families whose emotional style includes showering their members with shame through put-downs, insults, and blaming.

Identify two events/experiences about which you feel shame.

_____

_____

_____

Describe the connection between your using and feelings of shame.

_____

_____

_____

When the way you see yourself is "shame-based," anything you do that is less than exemplary reinforces the belief that you are defective and have been all along. In addition to reinforcing shame, addiction tends to be shame inducing, along the lines of "I have this problem so there's obviously something wrong with me." Shame is self-defeating to the point of being self-destructive and is an especially dangerous roadblock to recovery.

Describe how feelings of shame can be a potential roadblock to your recovery (be specific).

_____

_____

_____

Guilt is emotional distress or discomfort based on the belief that there is a problem related to your behavior, rather than you as a person. It is ordinarily related to a specific action or an event. "Authentic" guilt can be healthy and helpful insofar that it's a sign that we've violated our own values or a more universal moral code. It helps keep us honest and self-aware in ways that contribute to emotional balance.

In contrast, "false" guilt is a sense of responsibility for things that go wrong, for which we are not responsible. It is easy to fall into a pattern of guilt-driven self-blame—for not being able to stop using; for being an addict; for not being able to work or perform other physical activities as before, etc.

Identify two events/experiences about which you feel guilt.

1. _____

_____

_____

2. _____

_____

_____

Describe the connection between your using and feelings of guilt.

_____

_____

_____

Describe how feelings of guilt can be a potential roadblock to your recovery (be specific).

_____

_____

_____

LONELINESS AND ISOLATION

Loneliness, and the tendency to act on it by isolating oneself from other people, is frequently connected to depression, sadness, grief, and loss. Loneliness is defined as a state of sadness due specifically to the emotional experience of being disconnected from others and of feeling and/or being alone. This feeling may come from a sense of being alone with the disease of addiction, and that no one understands or can understand your situation. The experience of loneliness can be so consuming that some have described it as feeling utterly alone, even in a crowd of people.

Describe the three most common ways you isolate from others.

1. _____

_____

2. _____

_____

3. _____

_____

Loneliness is also often a problem for people in active addiction because over time, the progression of using intensifies a self-centeredness that further separates you from other people. You may use to block out feelings of loneliness, but using only alienates you more from family, friends (with the exception of using friends who are also increasingly self-centered), and the world as a whole.

Describe the connection between your using and feelings of loneliness.

_____

_____

_____

Describe how feelings of loneliness can be a potential roadblock to your recovery (be specific).

_____

_____

_____

Stressing Out

Stress can play a major role in beginning involvement with drugs and/or activities and continuing that involvement. For people in recovery, stress is frequently involved in the process of relapse. Many people describe using in response to stress, and stress is a common rationalization/justification to use: "I'm only using because I'm under so much stress." "I need to take the edge off." "It helps me relax." "If you were under as much stress as I am, you'd use too!" Because everyone experiences stress, difficulty handling it can present a fundamental roadblock to recovery.

Stress is talked about extensively, but what exactly is it? Stress is an imbalance between your current coping abilities and the expectations or demands that are placed on you, including demands that you place on yourself—both internally and externally, real and perceived. Stress affects the mind and the body in direct and powerful ways.

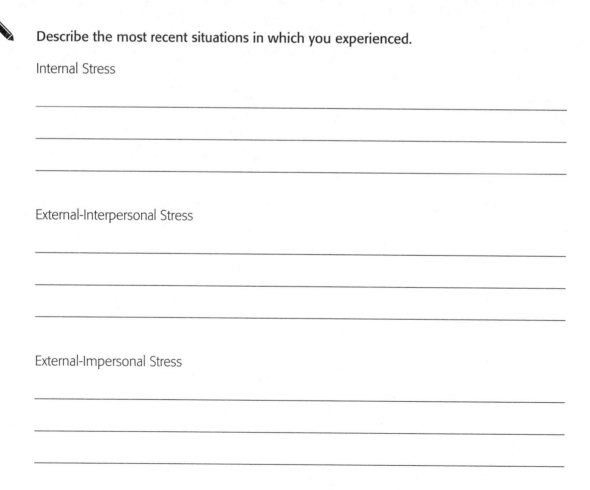

Stressors: Situations/Factors Contributing to Stress

Internal: Primarily "self-inflicted" based on self-imposed expectations, values, or standards that you (e.g., perfectionism) or others (e.g., other people are supposed to behave a certain way) "should" or "must" maintain.

External Interpersonal: Based on interactions and relationships with others—tension, conflicts/arguments, abuse, or violence between people who know one another.

External Impersonal: Environmental—weather, natural disasters, wars, random acts of violence, etc.

Describe the most recent situations in which you experienced.

Internal Stress

_____

_____

_____

External-Interpersonal Stress

_____

_____

_____

External-Impersonal Stress

_____

_____

_____

Stress automatically and unconsciously activates the systems in your body that are involved when quick response and rapid action are required. These include survival-oriented "fight, flight, or freeze" reactions to perceived threats.

> Stress automatically and unconsciously activates the systems in your body that are involved when quick response and rapid action are required.

These fight, flight, or freeze stress reactions are your body's way of protecting you. However, beyond a certain point, stress stops being helpful and becomes a substantial roadblock to recovery, interfering with your health, your thinking and mood, your relationships, your ability to be productive, and your overall quality of life.

Symptoms of Excessive Stress

Mental—forgetfulness, cynicism, negativism, self-criticism

Emotional—irritability, low frustration tolerance, decreased empathy

Physical—fatigue, tightness of neck or back, stomach aches, headaches

Behavioral—interpersonal conflict, proneness to accidents, decreased productivity, sleep disturbance (increased or decreased sleep), appetite disturbance (eating more or less), decreased involvement with others, or isolation

Your body's response doesn't know the difference between physical and emotional threats or between dangers that are real or imagined. When you're stressed over a busy schedule, an argument with a friend, coworker, partner or child, a traffic jam, or your monthly bills, your body reacts essentially the same way as it would if you were facing a life-or-death situation that required flight or fight. The more fear, anxiety/worry, and responsibilities you have, the more your emergency stress response is switched to "on." The more time your body's stress system is activated, the harder it is to shut off.

 Describe your primary stress symptoms.

Mental

_____

_____

Emotional

_____

_____

Physical

_____

_____

Behavioral

_____

_____

Describe the connection between stress and your using.

_____

_____

_____

_____

Describe how getting clean and being in recovery may be stressful for you.

_____

_____

_____

_____

Chronic, ongoing exposure to stress—regardless of whether you are in actual physical danger or simply *feel* like you are—negatively affects nearly every system in your body. It can raise your blood pressure, suppress your immune system, increase your risk for heart attack and stroke, and speed up the aging process. Like other repetitive experiences, long-term stress can even rewire the brain, leaving you more vulnerable to fear, anxiety, depression, and yes, stress.

Describe how stress can be a potential roadblock to your recovery (be specific).

_____

_____

_____

_____

_____

Connecting the Dots between Stress and Trauma

Stress becomes especially harmful when the body's stress response stays activated or stuck in the "on" position as a result of traumatic incidents—particularly when those incidents are ongoing or of especially high intensity. This is what happens with post-traumatic stress—the body's stress response system is always on.

Toxic and post-traumatic stress can emerge in the face of continuous family chaos or conflict, persistent emotional abuse, physical and/or sexual abuse, chronic parental depression, persistent parental addiction, and continuing emotional or physical neglect.

A stressful event is most likely to be traumatic if:

- It happened unexpectedly.
- You felt powerless to prevent it.
- It involved intentional cruelty.
- You were unprepared for it.
- It happened repeatedly.
- It happened in childhood.

Adding Injury to Injury: Unresolved Trauma

Please note: If you've gone through a traumatic experience, you may be struggling with upsetting emotions, frightening memories, or a sense of being unsafe that seems to follow you around. Or you may feel numb, disconnected, and have difficulty trusting other people. These are common reactions to trauma. In the event that this section brings up anxiety, fear, and/or anger that are difficult for you to handle, it is important for you to be conscious of your reactions and talk about them with someone you can trust and with whom you feel safe. You can distinguish between "there and then" and "here and now," between the past and the present.

Trauma is the result of extraordinarily stressful events that disrupt your sense of safety and security and lead to feelings of vulnerability and helplessness. When people think of trauma it is common to think of the traumatic experiences of our soldiers in Iraq and Afghanistan, or the thousands of people who are survivors of civil wars, or natural disasters such as hurricanes or tsunamis. Shootings on college campuses or in corporate offices also leave behind many trauma survivors.

Traumatic experiences often involve a threat to life or safety, but any situation that leaves you feeling overwhelmed and alone can be traumatic, even if it doesn't involve physical harm. Unresolved trauma festers like an infection and can contribute to self-defeating belief systems and low self-esteem, resulting in poor decision-making and problems in intimate relationships. It is a considerable roadblock to recovery.

Trauma can be caused by one-time events, such as a horrible accident, natural disaster, or a violent attack. As noted above, it can also result from ongoing, intense stress, such as living in a crime-ridden neighborhood or struggling with cancer. The majority of people who are traumatized experience insidious and chronic forms of trauma that often occur within their own family system. More obvious forms of trauma in the family include being subjected to and/or witnessing physical and sexual abuse. It may be more subtle, perhaps involving living with fear on an ongoing basis—such as the fear of not knowing *if* or *when* a parent is coming home or the fear that comes with listening to one's parents argue night after night.

It is not the objective facts about an event that determine whether it is traumatic, but rather your subjective emotional experience of that event. The more frightened

> Unresolved trauma festers like an infection and can contribute to self-defeating belief systems and low self-esteem…

and helpless you feel, the more likely you are to be traumatized. That's why childhood trauma increases the risk of future trauma. Traumatic experiences in childhood can have a severe and long-lasting effect. Children who have been traumatized see the world as a frightening and dangerous place. When childhood trauma is not resolved, this basic sense of fear and helplessness carries over into adulthood setting the stage for further trauma.

TRAUMA SYMPTOMS

Following a traumatic event, most people experience a wide range of emotional and physical reactions. These are essentially normal reactions to abnormal events. Such symptoms may last for weeks, months, or even years after the trauma ends.

Trauma survivors often try to quiet their distress by using substances—including food or activities. Frequently their use of substances or high-risk behaviors increases in response to anxiety or depression. It is common to see both addiction and co-occurring mental health disorders related to anxiety and depression in people with histories of significant trauma.

Emotional symptoms of trauma include shock, denial, or disbelief; anger, irritability, mood swings; guilt, shame, self-blame; distressing memories or thoughts about the event(s); feeling sad or hopeless; confusion, difficulty concentrating; anxiety and fear; and feeling disconnected or numb.

Physical symptoms of trauma include insomnia or nightmares; being startled easily; hyper-vigilance (consistently being on guard and on the lookout for possible danger); withdrawing from others; racing heartbeat; aches and pains; fatigue; edginess and agitation; and muscle tension.

Looking at your life, what traumatic experiences have you been through? (Remember, trauma can be a huge one-time event, a few big events, or much more subtle ongoing experiences in one's family or community.)

_____

_____

_____

_____

_____

If you've experienced trauma, describe your primary trauma symptoms.

Physical symptoms of trauma

_____

_____

Emotional symptoms of trauma

_____

_____

Describe how trauma can be a potential roadblock to your recovery (be specific).

_____

_____

_____

_____

_____

Taking Medication

When people take medication in response to medical/chronic pain and mental health conditions, they face additional recovery roadblocks. For those with addiction, taking mood-altering medications is always a slippery slope with serious risks. It is impressively easy to rationalize taking such medications in higher doses or more often than the prescriptions call for or than is necessary. It is natural for them to minimize the significance of misusing medications and deny that it is a potential problem. In fact, for people in recovery taking medication can be so problematic that it is often a pathway back to active addiction.

Please be advised that medical conditions, including chronic pain, should always be assessed by medical professionals, ideally by those who are familiar with addiction. When addiction co-occurs with mental health conditions, such as schizophrenia, bipolar disorder, PTSD, significant depression and/or anxiety, assessment by behavioral health professionals who are also knowledgeable about addiction is essential.

> The only way to know the true nature of medical and mental health challenges with accuracy—separate from the effects of your active addiction— is to have a comprehensive assessment *after* the post-acute withdrawal process has run its course (depending on how much and how long you've used, this can take several weeks to three or even six months).

Because the effects of active addiction can look like, as well as contribute to symptoms of, medical or mental health conditions, it is extremely important professional assessments take into consideration the potential impact of post-acute withdrawal. Remember, during post-acute withdrawal your body and brain are rewiring themselves as you adjust to being abstinent from the manifestations of your addiction. Difficulties in thinking, concentration, attention span, judgment, memory, sleep, appetite, and mood—including anxiety, irritability, and depression—are common.

Some people in recovery have a legitimate need to take some form of antianxiety and/or antidepressant medication. However, it is important to be aware that such medications tend to be overprescribed (especially by physicians who have less understanding of addiction) and taken much more often than is necessary. Taking antianxiety and sleeping medications in particular, can lead to relapse and back to active addiction.

Many people experience the challenges of chronic pain. Pain is the most frequent reason that Americans seek medical attention. Chronic pain has many unhealthy effects, including but not limited to: damage to relationships; job/career and financial problems; poor/damaged self-image; and feelings of isolation or being trapped, anxiety, fear, anger, and depression.

Opioid medications are the primary form of treatment for chronic pain. It is helpful to know that opioids are highly addictive—they are part of the same class of drugs as heroin and morphine. In fact, heroin was originally developed as a medication to treat pain in the mid-1800s. In addition to their potential for addiction, opioids have a number of other negative side effects.

Painkillers, as opioids are often called, cause clouded thinking and impaired mental functioning; lethargy; sleepiness; deficits in attention, concentration, and memory; feelings of irritability and depression; chronic constipation; and sleep disturbances. Withdrawal from them creates considerable anxiety and physical discomfort.

In spite of the significant risks for people with histories of addiction, many utilize a variety of rationalizations to justify using medically prescribed opioids. After all, they need to relieve their pain, it's legal, and it *is* recommended by a doctor—any "high" they experience is simply a "bonus."

For additional information on chronic pain, the connections between chronic pain and addiction, and pain recovery, you may be interested in reading:

A Day without Pain (Revised Updated Edition). Mel Pohl, MD, DFASAM (Central Recovery Press, Las Vegas, NV, 2011).

Pain Recovery: How to Find Balance and Reduce Suffering from Chronic Pain. Mel Pohl, MD, DFASAM; Frank J. Szabo, Jr., LADC; Daniel Shiode, PhD; Robert Hunter, PhD (Central Recovery Press, Las Vegas, NV, 2009).

Some Assembly Required: A Balanced Approach to Recovery from Addiction and Chronic Pain. Dan Mager, MSW (Central Recovery Press, Las Vegas, NV, 2013).

Ironically, the ongoing use of opioids can actually cause more pain via a phenomenon known as *opioid-induced hyperalgesia*. This often affects people with chronic pain who are on opioids long-term and have developed tolerance to lower dosages, rendering the medication less effective. Unfortunately, ever-increasing doses of opioids only reduce pain briefly before the effects of opioid-induced hyperalgesia increase it again.

Refusing to Part Ways with People, Places, Events, and Things

In recovery, you are advised to avoid the people, places, and things (events or objects in your environment) that have been associated with your active addiction. In active addiction, you learned to connect certain experiences and situations with using. Consequently, re-experiencing such people, places, and things can set off the vicious circle of obsessive thinking, compulsive behaving, and self-centeredness that make you extremely vulnerable to using.

These are sometimes referred to as "old playmates, playgrounds, and playthings" and include:

- The people—with whom you used, who helped you use, or who you "copped" from.

- The places—the part of town, block, street, corner, houses, or other locations—associated with your using or where you know people who use.

- The events, like parties, dinners, birthdays, holidays, or other celebrations, where you used or at which the manifestation(s) of your addiction are available.

- The objects/activities that were involved in your using, such as money, particular types of sex or sex partners, using paraphernalia, music, etc.

> In recovery, you are advised to avoid the people, places, and things (events or objects in your environment) that have been associated with your active addiction.

- Other experiences and situations like certain times—days of the week, weekends, specific times of the year during which you feel internal or social pressure to use.

The inability or refusal to accept the need to stay away from these old playmates, playgrounds, and playthings and part ways with them is a critical roadblock to recovery.

> If you used to drink regularly at the corner bar, then going there to drink soda or water and hang out with your former-drinking partners will put you at great risk of using. Similarly, if you want to stay in recovery, it is not a good idea to go to the places where you used to get high or gamble simply to hang out and soak in the atmosphere.

Because of the ways the repetitive experiences of active addiction have created changes in brain structure and functioning, addicts have become conditioned to the people, places, events, and things connected to the manifestation(s) of their addiction. As a result, when you come in contact with any of them, your brain releases specific chemicals, like the neurotransmitter dopamine that activates the brain's reward center and stimulates a powerful desire to use. As the twelve-step saying suggests, "If you hang out around the barbershop long enough, eventually you'll get a haircut."

Sometimes people in recovery try to "test" themselves by being around the people, places, or things associated with the manifestation(s) of their addiction. Testing your self-control in this way is like playing Russian roulette. If you want to continue or resume your cycle of active addiction, the most effective plan is to spend as much time as possible with the people, places, and things connected to the manifestation(s) of your addiction.

If using formed the basis of your relationship with some "friends," then continuing to be involved with them will make it that much more difficult for you to stay in recovery. Of course, avoiding the people connected to your using is more complicated when they are family members, roommates, or coworkers. Such circumstances can present especially challenging roadblocks.

Staying in recovery often means that certain activities you participated in for fun and pleasure during your active addiction, the people with whom you participated, and perhaps even your lifestyle or a part of your identity, need to change. Two natural consequences of this change are boredom and loss. Boredom is related to the empty spaces left behind by the items and ideas you give up. Loss involves the people, places, events, and things that were associated with your active addiction and are no longer available to you if you want to stay in recovery. As described earlier, grief is a natural emotional state attached to loss.

Identify the people connected to your active addiction you need to part ways with for the sake of your recovery.

_____

_____

_____

_____

Identify the places connected to your active addiction that you need to part ways with for the sake of your recovery.

_____

_____

_____

_____

Identify the events connected to your active addiction that you need to part ways with for the sake of your recovery.

_____

_____

_____

_____

Identify the other objects and ideas, connected to your active addiction, that you need to part ways with for the sake of your recovery.

_____

_____

_____

_____

Describe how not parting ways with these people, places, and things can be a roadblock to your recovery.

_____

_____

_____

_____

_____

Thinking in Distortions and Clinging to Faulty Beliefs

Beyond the people, places, events, and things that are connected to the manifestation(s) of your addiction, the thoughts and beliefs you have about these and other situations can also present challenging roadblocks to your recovery.

The defenses of denial, minimization, and rationalization are connected to distortions in thinking and faulty beliefs. Common examples of distorted thinking that lead to faulty beliefs include:

- thinking you can continue to hang out with your using friends and believing it won't have a negative impact on your recovery;

- thinking you can have alcohol in your home to serve to visitors and believing you won't be drawn to it; and

- thinking you can attend parties or other events where the manifestations of your addiction are available and believing you are "strong enough" to handle it.

Whenever you experience something—anything—whether it is positive or negative, you will always have thoughts about it *before* you *feel* the feelings. These thoughts often happen so quickly and automatically that you are often not even consciously aware of them. It is the way you think about the situation and your beliefs about it—how you interpret it—that creates your emotional response to how you feel about *it.* Your emotional response—the way you feel about something (whatever *it* is)—has great influence over your actions/behavior.

Although many people experience distortions in thinking and faulty beliefs that go along with them, for those with addiction there are special risks that represent potential roadblocks to recovery. Some thought distortions and faulty beliefs create intense negativity and contribute directly to uncomfortable, painful, upsetting feelings, which in turn, lead to increased stress and physical discomfort and result in a higher risk of using specifically to feel better.

What usually happens is that when your thoughts and beliefs related to a particular situation are distorted toward the negative, the emotions that result usually include: frustration, anger, anxiety, fear, self-pity, guilt, shame, sadness, and depression. There is a correlation between negative thinking and beliefs and the level of these emotions you experience—the more negative your thoughts and beliefs, the more intense and uncomfortable the feelings. And the more intense and overwhelming your feelings, the stronger will be your desire to escape from or numb them, and in turn, the more likely it is that you will use.

This can easily and quickly become a vicious circle as follows:

An experience—external or internal > distorted negative thoughts and faulty beliefs > feelings of frustration, anger, self-pity, anxiety, fear, guilt, shame, sadness, and/or depression > stress and physical discomfort > increased negative thoughts and beliefs > greater feelings of frustration, anger, self-pity, anxiety, fear, guilt, shame, sadness, and/or depression, and so on.

The longer such a cycle continues, the more you are at risk for relapse. There are a variety of specific types of distortions in thinking.

DISCOUNTING THE POSITIVE

When you discount the positive, you find ways to ignore, filter out, dismiss, or otherwise not be aware of anything remotely positive with regard to the matter at hand, whatever it may be. You choose instead to focus your conscious attention and energy on the negative aspects of the situation. This thought distortion colors your thoughts, feelings, potential options, and actions in negative ways.

For example, ten people tell you how well you seem to be doing, while a single person tells you, for whatever reason, that you don't seem to be doing well. Rather than believe the ten people with positive views, you are certain the one negative perspective is correct. In addition to feeding your negativity, this can also serve the self-defeating purpose of confirming what you believe about yourself—that you are not doing well. What do those other ten people know anyway?

Describe a situation when you have engaged in discounting the positive.

_____

_____

_____

If you were to engage in discounting the positive thinking, now or in the future, with what issue(s) would it most likely happen?

_____

_____

_____

Describe specifically what form it would take (describe your thought process).

_____

_____

_____

_____

_____

MAKING MOUNTAINS OUT OF MOLEHILLS

This distortion occurs when you take a small problem and make it much worse in your head by how you think about it. Perhaps you sense a problem or even a *potential* problem, and start thinking the sky is falling and the worst-case scenario is inevitable. You experience a situation that may be uncomfortable for you, but in the larger picture is not that big of a deal. However, your thoughts tell you, *This is horrible!* Your beliefs insist, *The only way I can deal with this is to use!*

For instance, you're driving to an appointment and get a flat tire. You have to go through the process of changing the tire or you have to call for assistance. If the weather is lousy it means having to deal with that as well. Of course, it's stressful and inconvenient, and it means that you will be late or perhaps miss your appointment, but you're okay. Still, your thoughts keep saying that this is grossly unfair, and you shouldn't have to deal with it. Your thoughts become fuel for frustration, self-pity, anger, and maybe even rage. The longer this process continues, the better using begins to sound.

You can blow the situation out of all reasonable proportion as you get caught up in spinning elaborate scenarios related to events that probably will never actually occur. You can spend considerable time and emotional energy looking for potential trouble, as well as solutions to problems that don't exist.

Describe a situation when your thinking has turned a molehill into a mountain.

_____

_____

_____

If you were to engage in making mountains out of molehills thinking, now or in the future, what issue(s) would it most likely happen with?

_____

_____

_____

Describe specifically what form it would take (describe your thought process).

_____

_____

_____

_____

BLACK-AND-WHITE THINKING

Thinking in "black-and-white" or "either/or" terms, where your thoughts, ideas, or objects are at opposite extremes from one another with nothing in between, creates imbalance in thinking by viewing events, situations, and people (including yourself) in one of only two mutually exclusive ways: all good or all bad. Everything is either "magnificent" or it's "terrible." Self-perception tends to be based on the extremes of "I am perfect"/"I am a total failure," "I am better than everyone else"/"I am worse than everyone else," or "I am in constant anger, fear, anxiety"/"I must be entirely free of anger, fear, anxiety."

Your thinking can also shift from one extreme to the other, depending on circumstances. In this thought pattern there is no middle ground. In fact, most of reality occurs somewhere in the middle, in the gray area between the extremes of black and white. When you are unable to see and appreciate this middle ground within the many possible shades of gray, you miss much of the richness and subtlety of life.

Describe a situation when you have engaged in black-and-white thinking.

_____

_____

_____

If you were to engage in black-and-white thinking, now or in the future, what issue(s) would it most likely happen with?

_____

_____

_____

Describe specifically what form it would take (describe your thought process).

_____

_____

_____

_____

_____

THINKING IN "SHOULDS"

Everyone has beliefs about how life *should* be—related to themselves, to others, and to the world. However, when you use the word "should" in your thinking, it creates a sense of expectation along with the internal pressures that go hand-in-hand with expectations. Sometimes these expectations become imperatives such as "My life must be this way or it must be the way I want it to be." "Shoulds" usually involve judging ourselves, others, and situations against specific standards for behavior and reality that we've created in our minds.

Whenever you think in terms of how people or situations should be, you set yourself up for disappointment. When you don't perform as you think you should; when others don't act as you think they should; or when situations don't turn out as you think they should; the resulting emotions are likely to include guilt, shame, frustration, hurt and/or anger. For addicts struggling with letting go of people, places, events, and things associated with their active addiction, this distortion can create imbalances in thinking along the lines of *It's not fair that I can't hang out with my old friends. I should be able to do all that I used to do. I shouldn't have so much that I can't do!*

Describe a situation when you have engaged in thinking in shoulds.

_____

_____

_____

If you were to engage in thinking in shoulds, now or in the future, with what issue(s) would it most likely happen?

_____

_____

_____

Describe specifically what form it would take (describe your thought process).

_____

_____

_____

_____

_____

Having Unrealistic Expectations

Expectations consist of wanting and anticipating a specific outcome or result related to people or situations. Even realistic expectations that are reasonable and practical create the potential for disappointment when the hoped-for results do not become reality. An expectation becomes unrealistic when the outcome that is desired and anticipated is unreasonable, illogical, or irrational, given the situation. Consequently, the hoped-for result is simply not possible, or at least, highly unlikely.

> An expectation becomes unrealistic when the outcome that is desired and anticipated is unreasonable, illogical, or irrational, given the situation.

Unrealistic expectations are at best a set up for disappointment and at worst a set up for failure. The more unrealistic your expectations are, the greater your disappointment will be when they are not met.

When unrealistic expectations go unmet (as they almost always do), the disappointment and/or sense of failure that inevitably comes with them—often with distressing feelings of sadness, depression, upset, and anger—can act like a magnet, pulling you back toward active addiction.

Identify and describe your three biggest expectations related to recovery.

1. _____

_____

_____

2. _____

_____

_____

3. _____

_____

_____

Describe what it is about these expectations that make them realistic (be specific).

1. _____

_____

_____

2. _____

_____

_____

3. _____

_____

_____

Describe what it is about these expectations that may be unrealistic (be specific).

1. _____

_____

_____

2. _____

_____

_____

3. _____

_____

_____

People naturally have expectations in recovery exactly as they do in many areas of their lives. At first, your expectations may be exceptionally simple. You may realistically expect that if you participate in the ongoing, daily work of recovery, the quality of your life will gradually start to improve. However, if you expect that all of the problems created in your active addiction and the consequences of your past actions will somehow disappear, or that you will quickly be forgiven by all those you have hurt, or that recovery will make you immune to future problems, you are clearly being unrealistic.

Staying clean or abstaining from addictive behaviors one day at a time—or even one hour at a time—is a realistic goal. Expecting that you will absolutely, positively stay clean or abstain from addictive behaviors for the rest of your life is a set up for disappointment and failure. It is certainly possible that you will stay clean or abstain from addictive behaviors for the rest of your life, but you will have to do a huge amount of difficult and challenging work on yourself on a daily basis in order for that to happen. You may unrealistically expect that as soon as you complete detox or stop using you will feel noticeably better right away. Remember the earlier section on post-acute withdrawal?

Unrealistic expectations can also take the form of expecting the worst. Do you believe your life might as well be over if you can't use? Do you expect that it will be impossible to have fun in recovery? Do you expect that twelve-step meetings are a bunch of "losers" sitting around whining and complaining? Do you expect the twelve-step program of recovery to be some sort of cult that will try to convert you to a particular set of religious beliefs?

Unless you have learned how to predict the future, expectations always produce the potential for a frustrating letdown. Unrealistic expectations are a big roadblock to recovery.

Identify and describe two expectations related to your recovery that you now understand are unrealistic.

1. _____

_____

_____

2. _____

_____

_____

Floating on the Pink Cloud

The pink cloud is a phenomenon that can affect people in recovery, especially those in early recovery. This experience often creates a particularly powerful and seductive type of unrealistic expectation. Under the influence of the pink cloud effect, people are ecstatically enthusiastic about recovery, almost as if they are intoxicated by it. Such people seem to act as if they are seeing sunshine for the first time. For them, life in recovery is absolutely fantastic; they've never felt better; they love this life; they love everything about this new way of living; they embrace it wholeheartedly, and simply know this is going to last forever!

> Unfortunately, anyone who believes that they will always feel as good as they do under the pink cloud's influence is setting themselves up for serious disappointment.

Unfortunately, because people experiencing a pink cloud effect feel so much better, they are at high risk to stop doing the actual work of recovery. And many do discontinue their recovery process under the misguided belief that they are somehow cured. This is an especially hazardous recovery roadblock because, contrary to the feeling that it will last forever, the effects of the pink cloud are always temporary. In fact, they are usually extremely short-lived, typically lasting several days to a few weeks.

The pink cloud does provide a brief glimpse of the positive potential of life in recovery. Unfortunately, anyone who believes that they will always feel as good as they do under the pink cloud's influence is setting themselves up for serious disappointment. When you allow yourself to get carried away on this cloud without doing the work necessary to build a solid foundation of recovery, you risk a massive fall without a safety net, and the results are never positive. They often include relapse, and with it, the possibility of a full return to active addiction.

If you have experienced a pink cloud, describe what it was like and how it affected you.

_____

_____

_____

If you have yet to experience a pink cloud, what form do you think it will take? What do you think it would look like?

_____

_____

_____

_____

Becoming Complacent

Complacency is a roadblock that challenges almost everyone at some point in his or her recovery. **Complacency** refers to a sense of self-satisfaction combined with an unawareness of actual or potential dangers. When most life issues appear to be going smoothly—whether in life in general or in specific life areas (such as recovery)—it can be easy to begin to take the success for granted and become complacent. There is an almost natural tendency to become complacent in recovery when all is well and there are no crises demanding attention and providing motivation to take action.

Change is always hard. Rarely do people want to change, especially when it comes to making big changes in their lives. Moving from active addiction to recovery is a huge change. Change occurs when the discomfort and pain of the current situation gets to the point where it outweighs the anxiety and fear of making changes in that situation. Most addicts come to the realization that they need to change their lives only after their addiction has created serious

> Complacency is a roadblock that challenges almost everyone at some point in his or her recovery.

problems for them. They find the willingness to make the significant changes necessary to take them from active addiction to recovery only when they get to the point of having experienced intense pain. Sometimes this willingness is not entirely of one's own choosing and comes from such external sources as family, job, or law enforcement entities.

Many addicts describe coming to recovery after receiving the "gift" of desperation—their lives had reached the point where they *had* to do something different, and they were willing to do virtually anything to make that happen.

✎ **Identify and describe what motivated you to seek recovery (be specific).**

_____

_____

_____

_____

> The foundation for complacency in recovery is laid when addicts forget the potential for relapse is real and ever-present, no matter how well life may be going at the moment.

With the willingness that comes from a sense of desperation connected to the numerous negative consequences of active addiction, many addicts initially devote considerable time, attention, and energy to the work of recovery. Because they have the awareness that their lives (or at least, the quality of their lives) depend on it, they make recovery their highest priority and work on it daily. By attending twelve-step meetings, practicing meditation and prayer, establishing and using a support group, engaging in reading, writing/journaling, doing step work, developing a relationship with a sponsor, and attending any aftercare or other counseling needed to help them learn, grow, and heal, anyone challenged with addiction can improve the quality of their lives significantly.

The foundation for complacency in recovery is laid when addicts forget the potential for relapse is real and ever-present, no matter how well life may be going at the moment. In fact, complacency is most likely to set in when life in recovery is going smoothly, all is well, and you may begin to feel that after working hard to get where you are, you do not have to continue to work to maintain what you have. This can happen regardless of whether you are brand new to recovery or you have been in recovery for years.

Perhaps the wreckage left in the wake of your active addiction has started to clear and you are no longer experiencing any serious problems. Maybe you have been able to repair some relationships with family and friends and return to work. Possibly you are looking and feeling better than you have in a long time, and the memories of the negative consequences of your active addiction grow more distant with each passing week, month, or even year. And your awareness of the importance of making your recovery the priority it needs to be fades, along with your willingness to dedicate the time, attention, and energy it requires.

Your inner voice may have told you that you did not have a problem while in active addiction, even though after you experienced enough pain, you found that to be absolutely untrue. That same voice may be telling you that you are now fine and no longer have anything to be concerned about. So there's no need for you to spend so much time and energy on recovery; now you can focus on other issues.

Complacency is fed by the defenses of denial, minimizing, rationalizing, and avoidance. It can emerge and take many different forms at any point throughout the recovery process. When complacency takes hold, recovery takes more and more of a back seat to other priorities. This process can progress slowly, and so subtly that you have no conscious awareness of it.

> Relapse is not merely the act of using; it is a process that starts well before the actual use of one or more of the manifestations of addiction—often with a gradual return to the same kinds of thinking, ways of dealing (or not dealing) with feelings, and behaviors you demonstrated during your active addiction.

Complacency sets the stage for a return to active addiction, and signs of complacency can be easily hidden by defense mechanisms. However, the warning signs are there if you know what to look for.

The warning signs of complacency include, but are not limited to:

- Believing you have "completed" your recovery or that you are "recovered."

- Believing you "have this recovery thing down," and know everything you need to know, so there's no point in continuing the mental, emotional, behavioral, and spiritual pursuits that helped you get to this point in your recovery.

- Believing you no longer have a problem with addiction (perhaps with the encouragement of others) or that your amount of clean time somehow protects you from relapse.

- Disengaging from actively working on your recovery—discontinuing or significantly reducing meeting attendance and aftercare/therapy, meditating/praying, keeping in contact with your support group, journaling, reading, doing twelve-step work, or continuing to work with a sponsor.

- Engaging in thoughts, behaviors, and attitudes that were part of your patterns in active addiction, including returning, perhaps slowly and gradually, to being involved with "people, places, and things" associated with your using.

If you have experienced complacency, describe what it was like and how it affected you.

_____

_____

_____

If you have yet to experience complacency, identify and describe the two forms that complacency would be most likely to take for you.

1. _____

_____

_____

2. _____

_____

_____

Continuing Your Journey of Recovery

There are many potential challenges along the path of recovery. As a result, remaining abstinent and building your recovery requires you to be able to recognize them and learn to deal with them successfully. These challenges can present roadblocks that can obstruct your way. Some are distractions that divert your attention and energy away from your recovery, others are potholes that you can fall into and get stuck, and still others are steep cliffs that you can fall off and suffer serious injury and even death.

These roadblocks may get in your way temporarily or for a long time, depending on:

1. How clearly you see them.

2. How prepared you are when you encounter them.

3. How you respond to them.

The focus of this section has been to help you become more aware of many of the most common and critical challenges you can realistically expect to encounter along your path of recovery. With this awareness you can see potential roadblocks to your recovery much more clearly (#1). When you can see such roadblocks clearly you can prepare for them much more effectively (#2).

If you stop here, you will only be aware of the problem, not the solution. In other words, you may have a solid basic understanding of the problem of addiction and the different roadblocks to recovery, but little information and understanding of how to respond to them successfully (#3).

The next section will help you translate your growing awareness into action and construct a solid foundation of recovery you can continue to build on.

NOTES

_____

_____

_____

_____

_____

_____

_____

_____

_____

_____

PATHWAYS TO RECOVERY

Strategies, Suggestions, and Solutions To Strengthen Your Recovery

As noted earlier, recovery consists of two basic parts:

- Getting clean—discontinuing using, becoming abstinent, and stopping the vicious circle of active addiction.

- Staying clean—finding pathways to live without using and learning how to live a whole, healthy, and healed life.

Remember, getting clean is the easy part in that it only has to happen once. Staying clean is much harder because it's a continuous, daily process.

In *every* situation, there are choices to be made, and you get to *choose* how you will respond to the situations that life presents you. Everything that happened before is now in the past. That doesn't mean it's not important; it is helpful and healthy to understand and learn from your past. But, it does mean you can't change the past—both what you've done and what's been done to you. Each day presents new possibilities and the chance to make new and different choices. It is because you *can* change what happens to you in the present and the future that the most important questions facing you—no matter what the situation may be—are always:

- How will you respond to the situation you're in right here and now?

- What choices will you make going forward from where you are right here and right now?

What you choose to do will determine which gets stronger: your recovery or the potential for you to relapse back into active addiction.

Addiction frequently originates as a way to escape from, numb and, ultimately, avoid pain via mood-altering substances or behaviors that then becomes reinforced and habituated through the repetition of using. Such efforts to avoid experiencing emotional and physical pain may work temporarily, but

> Each and every time you get through a difficult situation, challenge, or problem without using, your recovery becomes a little stronger.

in the long run only end up creating more of it. Avoidance doesn't work because pain is an inevitable part of life. It is an essential aspect of being human. Everyone experiences uncomfortable, painful thoughts, emotions, and physical sensations. Avoiding pain is simply impossible. It is how we choose to respond to the emotional and physical pain we experience that determines whether we are able to get through that pain or we engage in addictive and/or other avoidance behaviors that extend and amplify it.

Many people may want recovery, or at least want the absence of the pain and suffering they experienced in active addiction. However, freedom from the pain and suffering of active addiction requires considerable effort. The pathways you learn and practice here may well be the keys that unlock the door to successful ongoing recovery for you. Recovery involves learning and applying solutions to the various challenges life will present to you. The more solutions you can learn that work for you, the better you will be able to deal with the different problems you may experience. Each and every time you get through a difficult situation, challenge, or problem without using, your recovery becomes a little stronger.

Recovering One Day at a Time

As twelve-step programs suggest, recovery truly does happen "one day at a time." This is a helpful reminder that you don't need to worry about not using for the rest of your life. It's not even helpful, especially in early recovery, to think about never using again, ever!

The idea of "never using again" tends to be so big that it's overwhelming. Those new to recovery sometimes become discouraged, anxious, angry, resentful, or scared, when they think about not using for the rest of their lives. You may be thinking, *There's no way I'm never going to use again, it's simply not possible!*

Guess what? Believe it or not, you don't need to worry about this. In fact, thinking about not using for the rest of your life is actually a waste of time and energy. The reality is that you only need to focus on not using *today*. You can neither change the past nor predict the future. As it relates to using, even thinking about tomorrow makes no sense in that it is not possible for you to use tomorrow until it arrives (unless you have learned how to bypass the space-time continuum and travel through time to the future). And when tomorrow arrives, it's now today.

Not using "just for today" is realistic and entirely possible. The idea of it is much less intimidating and much more attainable. Most importantly, you can do that. Sometimes, it may be helpful to break it down even further and concentrate on not using one hour at a time or even fifteen minutes at a time. It is important to know that by not using "one day at a time" people can put together many years of recovery and, as a byproduct of not using "just for today," end up never using again.

As detailed in Addiction and Its Manifestations, the brain adapts to repetitive (doing the same things over and over) experiences by forming memory tracks that are unconscious. The unhealthy repetitive experiences and behaviors of your active addiction led to certain changes in your brain and created specific memory tracks. Those memory tracks made it more likely you would think, feel, and act in ways that supported your using.

Fortunately, the human brain is extremely resilient and has the ability to heal and adapt to new and different repetitive experiences. You now have the opportunity to create memory pathways that support your recovery. By engaging in recovery-oriented experiences one day at a time, you can form a foundation of "habits" of recovery from these unconscious memory tracks.

It is important to know that by not using "one day at a time" people can put together many years of recovery and, as a byproduct of not using "just for today," end up never using again.

Practicing positive and healthy recovery-supportive habits has conscious, as well as unconscious impacts. Your deepening awareness will grow into self-awareness as you become more conscious of your own thoughts, beliefs, emotions, and actions, as well as how they are interconnected in ways that can block your recovery or help you build more pathways to it.

 Describe two actions you will take to stay clean today that can become part of your "habits" of recovery.

1. _____

_____

_____

2. _____

_____

_____

Filling the Internal Emptiness

Regardless of its specific form (alcohol or other drugs, gambling, eating, sex, etc.), addiction is an attempt to fill an internal hole or feeling of emptiness with something external. External things, such as substances, activities, material objects, money, or people may fill this hole, but only temporarily.

Once you stop using, the internal emptiness you've been trying to fill can seem to get even bigger. This is normal, natural, and understandable. Boredom is an indicator of this internal emptiness. The process of recovery includes learning and practicing ways to fill your internal emptiness that are positive, healthy, growth enhancing, and life-affirming. Recovery unfolds from the inside out.

When there is empty space, it will *always* get filled with something. If this internal emptiness is not filled in ways that are positive, healthy, and recovery-supportive, it will inevitably be filled in ways that are usually unhealthy and that you are familiar with, because anything that is familiar is naturally more comfortable. As a result, what is familiar to you has a powerful, natural, and understandable pull, almost like that of a magnet.

Identify two ways that are positive and healthy that you can practice to fill your internal emptiness.

1. _____

_____

_____

2. _____

_____

_____

Breaking In Recovery-Oriented Ways of Thinking, Feeling, and Acting

The process of getting and staying clean—of transitioning from active addiction to recovery—involves learning and practicing new and different recovery-oriented ways of thinking, feeling, and acting. This process is much like that of getting a new pair of shoes after having had the old ones for an incredibly long time. The old shoes fit like a glove; the fabric has molded itself to fit the shape of your feet precisely. They have been so comfortable for so long that you don't want to part with them; you want to hold on to them and continue to wear them.

But they no longer work for you. They are dirty and torn and have worn so thin that there are obvious holes. As a result, your feet often get cold and wet. The sole has no grip left so you slip and slide all over the place. It is clear to most everyone but you that your shoes are a mess and you need new ones.

But, you don't want new shoes; you like the ones you have just fine. You think, *If everyone would leave me alone and let me wear the shoes I want, everything would be fine*. But, deep down, you know otherwise.

Part of you desperately wants to hold on to the old shoes because you are so used to them and you can't imagine life without them, while another part of you knows the old shoes definitely aren't working any longer and you honestly do need new ones. Even still, you have fear about what life will be like without your old shoes. You think there is no way new shoes could possibly fit you as well or be as comfortable as your old ones.

Finally, your feet become so battered, bruised, and blistered that you can no longer deny you need new shoes.

There comes a tipping point where the pain of the familiar becomes greater than the fear of change. You bite the bullet and, perhaps with the help and support of family and/or significant others, you get new shoes.

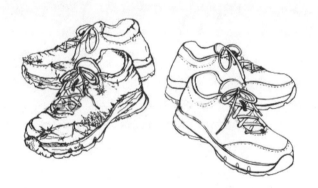

As is often the case with new shoes, at first they are unfamiliar and feel awkward. They're stiff and somewhat uncomfortable. However, if you can tolerate the initial discomfort and go through the process of practicing wearing the new shoes, gradually over time, they begin to feel more comfortable. The process of breaking-in new shoes does not happen as fast or as easily as you want it to. Yet, by continuing to wear them, one day at a time, it happens. Eventually, the new shoes become even more comfortable than the old ones. Moreover, they provide the support your feet needs and keeps them warm, dry, and healthy.

Connecting the Dots between Thoughts, Feelings, and Actions

In order to stay abstinent and in recovery, you are advised to avoid the "people, places, and things" that have been part of your using because they can easily get in the way of your continuing recovery process. The persons, locations, and items associated with using include the people you used with, the physical locations where drug use or addictive behavior occurred, and/or the activities, paraphernalia, etc. that are associated with active addiction. These are also sometimes referred to as "old playmates, playgrounds, and playthings."

In reality however, it isn't so much the people or situations that are so problematic, it's more about the challenges presented by:

1. The thoughts and beliefs you have about those people, places, and things.

2. How you handle the feelings that flow from your thoughts and beliefs.

3. What you do—how you act (your behavior) in response to your thoughts, beliefs, and emotions.

How you deal with these three areas—thoughts, feelings, and actions—determine whether you are sliding toward relapse or strengthening your recovery. The following section will help you gain a deeper awareness of how thoughts, beliefs, feelings, and actions are separate in certain ways yet ultimately interconnected.

> It is not events that cause feelings in people. It is the way those events are interpreted based on the thoughts and beliefs people have about them that bring up the feelings.

Following any event, people experience thoughts *before* they have any feelings toward it. It is the way you think about the event, your beliefs about it, and how you interpret it that actually determines your emotional response. Your emotional response (the way you feel about an event), in turn has substantial influence over your actions/behavior in response to it.

It is not events that cause feelings in people. It is the way those events are interpreted based on the thoughts and beliefs people have about them that bring up the feelings. In other words, feelings are not automatic in response to the events you experience; thoughts lead to, and in large part create, the emotions you feel, and the combination of your thoughts and feelings then lead to the actions you take.

This helps explain how different people can experience the exact same event and have entirely different feelings and behave in markedly different ways in response to it. Their thoughts and beliefs about the same situation can be absolutely different.

Here is how this process works: an **event** occurs—you experience something—it can be internal (coming from inside you) or external to you, such as physical pain or illness, the weather, traffic, a conversation or other interaction with someone you know or a stranger, conflict in your family or at work;

Which lead to **thoughts**—the way you *think* about the event; which lead to **beliefs**—the *meaning* you give to the event/the way you *interpret* it;

Which lead to **emotions**—the way you feel about the event; which lead to **actions**—the way you behave in response to your thoughts, beliefs, and emotions about the event.

As an example of this, let's say you see someone you know across the street and you wave to him or her. Even though this person is looking in your direction and seems to be looking directly at you, his or her facial expression seems to be irritated or angry, he or she doesn't wave back, and quickly walk away in a different direction.

Your first thoughts about this happening might go something like *He downright dissed me! How rude was that? Unfreakin' believable! How dare he treat me like that!*

These thoughts would likely lead to beliefs such as, *He disrespected me! What a jerk! I'm not going to simply take that! I don't deserve to be treated like that!*

 Take a moment and put yourself in that situation, having those thoughts, and the beliefs about the situation those thoughts lead to. What feelings would come up for you?

_____

_____

_____

Chances are, anger was one of the feelings you identified. Now, based on the feelings you identified, what actions would you take? How would you behave right after that event happened?

_____

_____

_____

And what would you do the next time you saw the person who didn't acknowledge you?

_____

_____

_____

What if instead, your first thoughts about the exact same event were, *I wonder what's up with him? How weird. It's not like him to not wave back.* These different thoughts would likely lead to different beliefs, such as *He must have been distracted or in a real rush. I hope he's okay. Maybe he didn't know it was me. Maybe he didn't see me waving to him.*

Now, take a moment, and put yourself back in that situation, having the second set of thoughts, and the beliefs about the situation those thoughts lead to. What feelings come up for you now?

_____

_____

_____

Chances are the feelings you identified were noticeably different the second time around. Based on this second set of feelings, what actions would you take with this person? How would you behave right after that event happened?

_____

_____

_____

_____

And with the second set of thoughts, beliefs, and feelings what would you do the next time you saw the person who didn't acknowledge you?

_____

_____

_____

Notice how directly your thoughts and beliefs about an event affect your feelings and, in turn, your actions. As this exercise makes clear your feelings and behavior flow from your thoughts and beliefs about an event. Thinking about events differently results in different beliefs, different feelings, and different actions.

Recovery and the Four Points of Balance

Active addiction is about extremes: it involves going from extreme highs to extreme lows, over and over and over again. Either life is fantastic or it sucks—it is all or nothing, either/or—there is no room for moderation and balance.

Balance between and within each of the four points is neither solid nor fixed; it is almost always in motion. You may find it helpful to think of it in terms of a seesaw or teeter-totter, a piece of play equipment once common to school yards and playgrounds. Typically, two children or groups of children sit on opposite ends of a wooden plank balanced in the middle riding up and down so that as one end goes down the other end goes up. The end that is up then goes down and the end that was down goes up in an alternating manner. Sometimes the movement of the seesaw is more extreme, going all the way up and then down, back and forth, at high speed; and sometimes, it is slower, more gradual, and softer.

When the up and down movement is intense and rapidly fluctuating it resembles the extreme mental, emotional, physical, and spiritual shifts that characterize active addiction. It can be thrilling, but there are serious potential threats to health and safety—it's easy to fall off or get hurt. When the movement is slower and gentler with milder ups and downs, it reflects what people are more likely to experience when they are in a process of recovery, consciously working toward mental, emotional, physical, and spiritual balance.

Although there may be brief periods when the seesaw is perfectly balanced, this never lasts long. The vast majority of the time there is some movement as the respective ends of the plank go up and down, sometimes slightly and subtly.

The same is true of mental, emotional, physical, and spiritual balance, even in recovery and under the best of circumstances—rarely does anyone achieve perfect balance, and when they do it is always temporary. As the circumstances of your life change, so will your state of balance.

Balance, like recovery from addiction, is a journey. Life's circumstances and events create challenges along the way. As opposed to viewing these challenges as obstacles, you are invited to see them as opportunities for learning and growing and healing. This journey is an ongoing process—it does

not have an end point. Striving for perfect balance, while an understandable goal, is simply not realistic. After all, life is rarely perfect. Every once in a while you may be blessed with brief experiences of what seems to you like perfection, but these moments are fleeting. In fact, focusing on achieving perfection can actually contribute to imbalance because it creates unnecessary stress and unrealistic expectations.

As you become aware of circumstances in your life that are out of balance, it is helpful to resist the urge to overcorrect through extreme or impulsive actions. There are no quick fixes. Changes are most healthy and effective when made gradually, yet progressively, taking into consideration all four points of balance: mental, emotional, physical, and spiritual. All four points represent the most essential aspects of being human and decades of scientific research on the mind-body connection has demonstrated they are all intimately linked to each other.

Whatever affects us mentally will also affect us emotionally, physically, and spiritually. Whatever affects us emotionally will also affect us mentally, physically, and spiritually. Whatever affects us physically will also affect us mentally, emotionally, and spiritually. And, whatever affects us spiritually will also affect us mentally, emotionally, and physically. Sometimes the ways in which the mental, emotional, physical, and spiritual affect each other is clear and direct, and other times it is more subtle and indirect. However, anything that affects one of these areas of your life—whether it is healthy and recovery-supportive or unhealthy and a potential recovery roadblock—will affect all of the others.

Mental Balance

Mental balance refers to our thoughts and our patterns of thinking—how we think about what we experience. Our thoughts and our way of thinking are generated from information from both internal and external sources. We then form interpretations and conclusions related to that information. This process can be conscious, but frequently it takes place unconsciously. Because our thoughts influence both our emotions and our actions, moving toward mental balance is essential to the process of recovery. More than anything else, mental balance is about becoming more consciously aware of your thoughts, paying attention to them and what they are telling you, and then questioning and challenging them as appropriate.

Not surprisingly, extremes of thought are common to people with addiction. Extreme thinking both contributes to active addiction and is one of the consequences of it.

EXTREMES OF THINKING

One extreme style of thinking is to virtually "skip over" thoughts entirely—in effect, to think too little. When your style is that of under-thinking, you are unaware of your thoughts. As a result, emotions are often expressed in uncontrolled and sometimes frightening ways. You may react to situations immediately, emotionally, and impulsively, rather than by thinking logically and acting based on consideration of the needs of the situation and selecting from available options.

Another extreme is to intellectualize situations—to think too much. If your style is one of overthinking, you will tend to be consumed by your thoughts. Ideas are king, and thinking is respected and even revered, while emotions are considered messy or unsafe, and their expression is suppressed, discouraged, minimized, or swept aside. You approach all situations intellectually and seek logical solutions, often to the neglect of appropriate emotional considerations. In extreme intellectualized thinking, excessive emphasis on thoughts and obsessive thinking about every possible option effectively paralyze decision-making and prevent necessary action from taking place.

Still another form of thinking in extremes is to believe that everything will be fine no matter what. This can be mislabeled as positive thinking, but it's truly a potentially dangerous way of thinking, that at its most imbalanced becomes denial. The pendulum of thought swings to the extreme of not seeing reality as it truly is, leading to consequences such as underestimating potential problems, ignoring negative realities, not taking care of yourself, and placing yourself in risky situations. For example, you truly don't see the nature of the drug problem that has developed.

On the opposite side of this extreme is another extreme: thinking that everything is lousy and always will be, regardless of what happens. Chronically negative thinking actually makes "bad" situations worse.

You may ruminate (go over and over a situation in your mind, replaying it unproductively) or magnify the negative, exaggerating the significance of something that occurred and turning what was only a small problem into a major disaster in your mind. By focusing so much on the negative aspects of your experience—for example, the problems created by your active addiction—you actually make your life more negative. Your thoughts have the capacity to make you miserable. Negative thinking can be especially insidious, feeding on itself, with the potential to become a self-fulfilling prophecy. Your thinking may or may not take you to these extremes, but having addiction typically includes experiencing various degrees of distorted, out-of-balance thinking.

> While you may be powerless over the automatic thoughts that first enter your mind, you are not powerless over what you do in response to them.

THINKING ABOUT THINKING

Have you ever considered why you think what you think? Does it seem like your thoughts are who you are? The reality is that nothing could be further from the truth. Your thoughts are part of you, but only a part of the much greater whole. In the seventeenth century, the French philosopher Descartes famously said, "I think, therefore I am." This statement represented an important step forward in the evolution of Western philosophy. However, in suggesting there is no separation between people and their thoughts, it has also done a disservice to our understanding of the relationship between our thoughts and who we are. Because they occur so automatically and seem so natural, we can become so closely identified with our thoughts that we believe there is no separation: Our thoughts are us and we are our thoughts. And yet, the reality is that we produce our thoughts. Thoughts are mental products generated in our brain.

Thoughts are like pictures on the video screen of the mind. The thought process that takes place before you feel any emotion or take any action usually happens so naturally, so quickly, and so automatically that you are not even consciously aware of it.

The first thoughts that come into your mind are like the channel that is on already when you turn on your television. While you may be powerless over the automatic thoughts that first enter your mind, you are not powerless over what you do in response to them. When you turn on your television and decide you don't like the channel that's on, you can change the channel to find something more to your liking. In the same way, you can observe your thoughts, question their accuracy, dispute or talk back to them, adjust them, and ultimately change them.

As you become more aware of your thoughts, you can begin to make conscious determinations as to how much credibility to give them and whether or not to believe what they are telling you. You can exercise the option of choosing to change them by thinking about events differently—basically changing the channel. Learning to become aware of your thinking and using that awareness to change or turn off thoughts of using or thoughts that provide fuel for using is not easy to do, but with practice it gets easier.

Scientific research continually generates increasing evidence of the intimate and inextricable connection between the mind and body. Whatever affects one will inevitably impact the other, regardless of where an identified problem originates. As a result, an imbalance in thinking can cause imbalances in emotional, physical, and even spiritual functioning. The knowledge that thinking can affect, and even change, feelings and behavior is not new. In fact, it has been around for thousands of years, having been a topic of discussion among the Stoic philosophers of ancient Greece and Rome. Moreover, we tend to believe in the inherent truth or accuracy of our thoughts. A variation on Descartes' revelation might be "I think it, therefore it is true." Our thoughts are influenced by upbringing (past conditioning), immediate environment (including external and internal experience), and enduring social and cultural messages.

Assuming our thoughts are facts—that they are all true and valid without examination—is one of the reasons we often find ourselves out of balance. This is particularly true when people are challenged with addiction.

As described previously, before emotion or action takes place in any situation, a thought process occurs. A thought process always takes place, but it can happen so quickly and automatically that the person is frequently not consciously aware of it. These seemingly natural, automatic thoughts are also known as "self-talk"—what we effectively tell ourselves about sensory events that also define our beliefs about those events. Again, while you may be powerless over the automatic thoughts or self-talk that may first enter your mind, you are not powerless over what you do in response to them. You can detach from them, observe them, question their accuracy, dispute or talk back to them, and ultimately, change them.

Your automatic thoughts and self-talk can have a huge influence over your feelings and behavior. In fact, the less aware of your thoughts you are, the more influence they have on your feelings and behavior. The more aware of your thoughts you become, the more choice you will have in how you act.

Becoming aware of your thought process and understanding it is essential to developing the ability to challenge it, and in turn, modify your emotions and the way you act in response to them. The more consciously aware of this process you can become, the more you will be able to develop the capacity to intentionally adjust your thinking and self-talk to respond to many situations in ways which are more helpful, healthy, and skillful.

Remember, since you have always thought in the particular manner in which you think, your way of thinking is similar to being on automatic pilot. Everything you think is not necessarily the truth or even accurate.

It is normal for your thought patterns to be so natural that you are not consciously aware of them. But in the process, you can also become unaware of how your thinking influences your actions and feelings about yourself and your place in the world. Paying attention to your thought process and consciously questioning and challenging your thinking is an indication of mental health and balance.

Those in recovery learn they are not what they think. We all have thoughts; however, we are not our thoughts. We can observe them and we can dispute them by not buying everything they are trying to sell us. Progress toward healing and recovery from addiction involves taking action on your thoughts. Instead of attempting to control your thoughts, healthy action is actually surrendering to the fact you cannot control your thoughts, but you can modify and redirect them in order to achieve balance.

NOTICING YOUR THOUGHTS

Recovery includes working on becoming consciously aware of your thought process to allow for acknowledgment and recognition of your thoughts without reacting to them automatically or impulsively. Observing your thoughts is the beginning of this process and will help you move toward balance. Instead of identifying your thoughts as indisputable facts, allow yourself to observe them with interest and curiosity. With practice, you will be able to witness your thoughts as they arise in your awareness.

Take a few moments and observe your thoughts as they come up for you right now. Write three that come to mind.

_____

_____

_____

_____

_____

> Take a little time each day to practice observing your thoughts.

DISPUTING YOUR ADDICTIVE THINKING

As discussed in the section on Roadblocks to Recovery, because addiction is addiction, once you are addicted to any drug, including alcohol, you are automatically at much greater risk of your addiction shifting to another drug or an activity, such as gambling, eating, sex, shopping/ spending, Internet use, and video gaming. This is true even if you are in recovery.

When you are addicted to any substance, crack, for example, you are at an extremely high risk for your addiction to cross over to alcohol or prescription pain medications or marijuana or any other substance you use.

Slowing down the thought process and not immediately and unconsciously reacting to perceived slights, insults or put-downs will help you move toward balance in this area. You can witness your thoughts as they arise in your awareness.

HOW SELF-DEFEATING THOUGHTS CREATE IMBALANCE

Imbalances of thought, wherein our mind approaches what is happening in our external reality in an inaccurate way, are common phenomena. Our minds have the responsibility and challenge of making sense of our experience in the world so that we can understand it. Depending on external circumstances and internal influences, the mind can easily make errors in interpreting our experiences, thus throwing us out of balance.

The mechanics of thinking can be significantly distorted by active addiction. The need to focus on getting the ways and means to use, using, and recovering from the acute effects of using, makes imbalanced thinking, twisted beliefs, and inaccurate interpretations of events and situations much more likely. The following sections focus on some common imbalances in thinking that many people who have struggled with addiction experience. Being aware of these self-defeating ways of thinking and learning, and practicing specific skills can help you pull yourself out of their grip.

DISCOUNTING THE POSITIVE

The stressors, pain, and problems of active addiction often result in negative thought patterns. One form these thoughts can take is to ignore, dismiss, or otherwise not be aware of anything remotely positive about a situation, whatever the situation may be. With or without your knowledge or your intent, you focus all your conscious attention and energy on the negative, unpleasant aspects of the situation.

For example, you hear from five different people how well you seem to be doing, while another person tells you, for whatever reason, that you don't seem to be doing well. Rather than believe the five people with positive views, you are certain that the one negative perspective is correct. In addition to feeding your negativity, this can also serve the self-defeating purpose of confirming what you may believe about yourself—that you are not doing well. We frequently find evidence in real events to support the position we've already taken.

In order to counteract this and re-establish balanced thinking, it is helpful to keep in mind that nearly all situations and events have both positive and negative characteristics. Sometimes you may have to look a little harder or even do some work to locate the positive, but if you put in the time and energy to look for it, you will find it. Another approach you can use to counteract this form of thinking is to identify things or people you are grateful for. Practicing the expression of gratitude can improve your mood and frame of mind, and measurably increase the experience of contentment.

SEEING THE POSITIVE

Describe a situation that only seems negative.

_____

_____

_____

Now take a closer look and identify some positive aspects about the same situation (these may include the lessons you can learn from it).

_____

_____

_____

_____

Identify three people or things that you are grateful for and briefly describe the reason(s) for your gratitude.

_____

_____

_____

_____

_____

MAKING MOUNTAINS OUT OF MOLEHILLS

Sometimes people have a tendency to get caught up in thinking that creates elaborate scenarios related to events that may never actually occur. They may spend considerable time and emotional energy looking for problems that don't exist and revving themselves up in the process. For instance, you sense pain in a specific area of your body that may be uncomfortable, but in the larger picture, is not that big a deal. However, your self-talk tells you, *This is horrible! It's going to spread to my entire body. I'll be in intense pain and have to miss time at work, school, etc.*

Thoughts that catastrophe is upon you or is inevitable has considerable influence on your perceived options and overall mental balance. The first step in interrupting this process is to become aware of it and realize what you are thinking. Only then can you make an informed decision about how you want and need to proceed based on the options available.

KEEPING THINGS IN PERSPECTIVE

Describe a situation where your thinking caused you to make it worse than it actually was.

_____

_____

_____

Describe how you can practice thinking differently so as not to make mountains out of molehills (be as specific as you can).

_____

_____

_____

_____

BLACK-AND-WHITE THINKING

Thinking in either/or terms, where circumstances are the complete opposite of each other with nothing in between, creates imbalance in thinking by viewing events, situations, and people (including yourself) in one of only two mutually exclusive ways: all good or all bad. Everything is either fantastic or it's horrible. Self-perception tends to be based on the extremes of *I am perfect / I am a total failure* or *I am great / I can't do anything right*.

Your thinking can also shift from one extreme to the other, depending on circumstances. In this thought pattern there is no middle ground. Yet, most of reality occurs somewhere in the middle, between the black and white and within those many shades of gray.

When you are unable to see and appreciate this middle ground, you end up missing much of the richness and subtlety of life.

You can regain balance by becoming consciously aware of this tendency, checking your thought process, and noticing when you are thinking in black-and-white terms. This awareness will provide the opportunity to look for the middle ground and the shades of gray you are missing.

SEEING THE SHADES OF GRAY

Describe a recent situation when you engaged in black-and-white thinking.

_____

_____

_____

Looking back at that situation, identify the shades of gray in it.

_____

_____

_____

_____

_____

SELF-ESTEEM/SELF-IMAGE

The progressive nature of addiction makes life smaller and smaller as you become more self-centered and your time and attention increasingly revolves around using. Many people with addiction experience financial, legal, or health problems, as well as problems related to jobs and career.

Most become less responsible as adults, and less physically and emotionally available as partners, as parents, and as children to their own parents. As these consequences accumulate, your self-image and self-talk can become increasingly negative and focus nearly exclusively on your losses and deficits. This may happen gradually enough that you are unaware of the changes in your thinking and the way you view yourself.

It is not unusual to be defensive about this and be unwilling or unable to admit to yourself and others how badly you are feeling about yourself. You may overcompensate by trying to be perfect at what you can do and pointing this out to others. Or you may withdraw, and even stop trying altogether, since having a "normal life" may seem impossible. The recovery process encourages you to look specifically at what you think and feel about yourself—your abilities, your limits, and what matters to you. This is part of the process of change that will lead you back to balance and the life you want to live.

You may have become so identified with your addiction that it becomes part of your core identity; you begin to think of yourself as a "victim," and emotional and physical pain becomes who you are rather than experiences you sometimes have. It's not unusual for people with addiction to come to define their sense of self in terms of their pain and impaired functioning. *I used to be able to do this or that* or *I used to provide better for my family* have roots in reality for some, but can also equate to *I am extremely weak* or *I'm no longer valuable to my loved ones*. Maintaining a balanced sense of self is essential to overall health. From a self-image standpoint, this might take the form of *I'm not a bad person trying to become good; I'm a sick person trying to become well. I'm working hard to change my life for the better, and I'm slowly but surely making progress. I'm grateful for what I can do. In spite of my challenges, I have the ability to have a meaningful life, and it begins with the way I think about myself.*

> The recovery process encourages you to look specifically at what you think and feel about yourself—your abilities, your limits, and what matters to you.

BROADENING YOUR SELF-IMAGE

Identify two changes you can make in your thoughts related to how you think about yourself.

_____

_____

_____

_____

EXPECTATIONS OF YOURSELF AND OTHERS

Everyone has beliefs about how life *should* be in relation to themselves, to others, and to the world. Expectations usually involve judging yourself, others, and situations against specific standards for behavior and reality that your thinking has created. Sometimes these expectations become imperatives, such as "Things *must* be the way I want them to be." Whenever you think in terms of how people or situations should be, you set yourself up for disappointment.

When you don't perform as you *think* you should; when others don't act as you *think* they should; when situations don't turn out the way you *think* they should; then the resulting emotions are likely to include guilt, shame, frustration, hurt, and/or anger. A solution to restore balanced thinking when you're caught up in expectations is to consciously separate what you may want from the reality of the situation. It's normal, natural, and understandable to want things the way you want them. But mental balance and recovery require you to develop the ability to accept the things you cannot change.

> It's normal, natural, and understandable to want things the way you want them.

Realistic expectations can slowly improve your ability to respond skillfully to the full range of circumstances life presents to you. If you do not use and practice monitoring and modifying your expectations, you will begin to gain a sense of greater mental balance. As the minutes become hours, and the hours become days, you will soon begin to let go of the fear, pain, disappointment, and a host of other negative emotions, which led you to use. The process can seem slow, but as you fulfill your expectations you will gain greater confidence in your ability to plan and to set realistic expectations.

Identify two changes you can make in your expectations of yourself that will help you move toward more mental balance.

_____

_____

_____

_____

Identify two changes you can make in your expectations of others that will help you move toward more mental balance.

_____

_____

_____

_____

Identify two changes you can make in your expectations for situations that will help you move toward more mental balance.

_____

_____

_____

_____

Emotional Balance

Emotional balance involves acknowledging and accepting your emotions, understanding that all feelings are neither good nor bad. People who have learned emotional balance know that trying to escape painful feelings may work temporarily, but in the long run it only prolongs those experiences and intensifies the suffering connected to them. Suffering is a function of the beliefs people attach to their emotional and physical pain—this is one of ways that how you think is directly linked to how you feel. For instance, whenever the belief exists that someone shouldn't be in pain and in turn, it is something to be avoided at all costs, that person will experience suffering. Ironically, the harder someone works to avoid the experience of pain, the greater his or her suffering tends to be. People who are balanced emotionally let themselves **feel their emotions, whether they are pleasurable or painful.**

GOING TO EMOTIONAL EXTREMES

The previous section detailed the connection between active addiction and uncomfortable feelings such as fear, anxiety, anger, resentment, depression, sadness, grief and loss, guilt, shame, loneliness, and isolation.

Although people often use (at least in part) to quiet painful emotions, over the course of time addiction has a way of creating significant imbalances in terms of how you experience feelings. These imbalances range from the extremes of feeling too much (emotional overreacting) to feeling too little (emotional underreacting).

Therefore, achieving emotional balance includes learning how to experience your feelings as they evolve without suppressing or "stuffing" them or being overwhelmed by or "drowning" in them. Statements that reflect these respective extremes range from *I don't feel anything; Nothing bothers me;* or *I feel numb;* to *I can't take it anymore! I want to stop feeling this way! or I hate feeling this way!*

Our style of emotional responding is a function of our past conditioning and life experience. The messages we received from our environment, dating from the time we were young children, regarding emotional expression, have significant impact on how we deal with feelings today.

Emotional underreacting is an emotional style that minimizes actual responses while avoiding or minimizing feelings and emotional expression. This can happen unconsciously or as a result of conscious decision-making. People with this emotional style rarely if ever seem to react with strong feelings. They keep their distance from emotions; they usually don't cry if someone dies (even those they may be extremely close to) and seem to treat virtually all situations as if nothing is a big deal. They learned early in life that expressing feelings is something to be avoided and, as a result, dealing with feelings directly—including actually *feeling* them—is unfamiliar, uncomfortable, and emotionally unsafe.

Emotional overreacting is on the opposite end of the spectrum. People with this style have minimal, if any, distance from the emotions they experience from one moment to the next. They express and often act out on their feelings immediately and impulsively.

They seem to be driven by emotions with little or no thought or logic. They tend to react to most situations as if they are true crises, living in and constantly creating drama. The urgency and intensity of this drama can have the effect of pulling other people in like a whirlpool and involving them in the scenario, whatever it may be. They don't just feel their feelings, but are consumed by them. Many people learned to overreact because they were raised in environments with that style, where emotions are expressed as soon as they are felt, without any conscious thought (literally thoughtless) about the potential consequences of instantaneous, sometimes reckless venting.

 In your emotional style, do you tend more toward underreacting or overreacting?

_____

_____

Describe how you underreact or overreact.

_____

_____

_____

If you were watching yourself underreacting or overreacting on a video screen, what would you see?

_____

_____

_____

_____

FEELINGS ALWAYS FIND A PATH TO EXPRESSION

It's human nature to want to avoid pain, including painful emotions, and most people struggling with addiction operate under the premise of maximum avoidance of emotional, as well as physical pain. An underlying belief is that pain—be it emotional or physical—is "bad" and needs to be avoided at all costs. A common thought process tells us that, if we can merely avoid the pain, it will disappear and won't affect us. However, in the same way that lightning will always find a path to ground, feelings always find a path to expression. If we do not address and express them consciously and directly by allowing ourselves to feel them and talk about them, if we avoid or suppress them, they will come out in indirect form via our behavior. When feelings are expressed through behavior, they are typically operating unconsciously and outside of our awareness and control.

> A common thought process tells us that, if we can merely avoid the pain,
> it will disappear and won't affect us.

It's similar to a pressure cooker. Balance is required inasmuch as a lid is necessary to keep the contents from spilling all over the place and making a massive mess, but a means to relieve pressure is also needed. When a pressure cooker is in operation, the pressure builds up inside. At some point this pressure needs to be released. The pressure requires a path to expression. If there is no release valve to provide a safe path to expression, what happens? The pressure builds until the vessel can no longer contain it and it explodes, causing potentially serious damage. In the same way, if we do not provide our feelings a safe (though at times uncomfortable) path to expression by feeling and talking about them consciously, they will still find a way out—often through some sort of unhealthy, self-defeating and/or explosive behavior.

By the time many addicts enter recovery they have become so accustomed to distancing themselves from their feelings with substances and avoidant behaviors that they describe not feeling anything other than numb or "bad." In recovery, people learn and begin to practice allowing themselves to effectively feel again.

The capacity to identify, feel, and express emotions in a balanced way is essential to health, well-being, and ongoing recovery. There are several levels of awareness and action involved in cultivating this capacity.

The first level is **becoming consciously aware that you are experiencing a feeling.** This awareness occurs when you first think about it or realize you feel something. Although you may not know specifically what the feeling is, it is important to definitely notice and acknowledge that you have *some* feeling.

The next step is to **identify the particular feeling.** A fundamental part of identifying your emotions is to put them into words. As an alternative to describing a mass of intense or vague feelings, it is helpful to say to yourself, "I feel anxious," or "I feel angry," or "I feel sad, depressed, fearful," etc. The more specific you can be in identifying your feelings, the clearer your understanding of your emotional experience will be. Moreover, the accurate identification of feelings enhances your ability to take the action(s) that are the best fit to meet your needs and support your recovery.

Take a moment and tune in to your feelings right now. Identify the specific feeling(s) you are experiencing.

_____

_____

_____

CONNECTING EMOTIONS TO BODILY SENSATIONS

A valuable approach to increase your emotional awareness and skills is to begin to make the connection between different emotions and where you feel them within your body. Learning how different emotions feel in your body in terms of their location (where you feel them) and sensation (what they feel like) will enable you to identify them more quickly and accurately.

Learning how different emotions feel in your body in terms of their location (where you feel them) and sensation (what they feel like) will enable you to identify them more quickly and accurately.

Read through the list of feelings in the left column of the table below and circle the ones you are experiencing. Next, take a moment to think. It may be helpful to close your eyes and turn your focus inward. Then, in the right column, indicate *where* you experience each feeling in your body. For example, anger might be felt as tightness in your shoulders, sadness as an aching in your chest, fear as a knot in your stomach, and joy as warmth in your heart.

Emotion(s)	Where and How You Feel It in Your Body
Frustration/Anger/Resentment	
Anxiety/Fear	
Sadness/Depression	
Loneliness/Isolation	
Guilt/Shame	
Grief/Loss	
Mixed Emotions/Ambivalence	
Confusion/Uncertainty	
Embarrassment	
Self-pity	
Gratitude/Appreciation	
Empathy/Compassion	
Love	
Joy	
Other: _____	

FEELINGS AREN'T FACTS AND THEY ARE ALWAYS TEMPORARY

In the same way our thoughts are not facts, neither are our feelings. They are simply our emotional response to our experiences, the thoughts our minds generate about those experiences, and our beliefs about them. As you have learned through previous exercises, when your thoughts about something change, so do your feelings. Different interpretations of your internal and external experiences lead to different emotional responses.

When we are caught up in our feelings—especially powerful distressing ones such as anxiety, fear, sadness, depression, guilt, shame, frustration, anger, loneliness, and grief—they sometimes seem as though they will last forever. However, whether they are positive and bring smiles to our face and laughter to our lips or painful and bring tears to our eyes, feelings are *always* temporary. Whether the feelings last for minutes that seem like hours, hours that seem like days, days that seem like weeks, or weeks that seem like months, they will not continue indefinitely—eventually they will change. As is said in twelve-step recovery programs, "This too shall pass."

Dealing with painful, uncomfortable feelings is similar to being mired in quicksand. The more you fight, the harder you struggle to get free, the more stress and tension you create, the deeper you sink and the more stuck you become. When you stop judging and struggling and allow what is there to simply be, you can free yourself. Painful feelings lose their grip and begin to dissipate on their own. This response is comparable to when you become consciously aware that you have been tightly clenching your jaw and then you stop clenching it. You immediately feel the tension in your jaw lessen and the muscles in your face begin to relax.

> When we are caught up in our feelings—especially powerful distressing ones such as anxiety, fear, sadness, depression, guilt, shame, frustration, anger, loneliness, and grief—they sometimes seem as though they will last forever.

Learning to be present-centered with your feelings by accepting them and simply letting them be without reacting to or acting on them is key. Remembering that all feelings are neither facts nor forever can increase your ability to observe and accept them, however uncomfortable they may be. This acceptance has an emotionally corrective healing quality.

As much as we would like to avoid it, the reality is that discomfort and pain are inevitable. We can't avoid pain, but we do have a choice in how we respond to our painful emotions. At some point, you realize that you only add more pain and suffering to your life and the lives of those closest to you when you overreact or allow your painful feelings to be expressed through your behavior.

In recovery, you have the opportunity to learn and practice consciously acknowledging, feeling, and expressing your emotions without further damaging yourself or those you care about. It is valuable to keep in mind that feelings are neither "good" nor "bad"; they simply are. Learning how to be okay with uncomfortable emotions and allowing yourself to feel them is known as **distress tolerance.** Given how many people relapse as a result of their inability to cope with painful feelings, learning the skills of distress tolerance is extremely valuable.

We invite you to begin to view your emotional reactions in the context of whether they are appropriate and in proportion to the situation at hand, and to what extent how you handle your feelings moves you in the direction of greater balance. Accepting your feelings takes much less energy than trying to deny or suppress them, thus allowing you to shift your energy to more productive pursuits. With emotional balance you feel your full emotional experience, recognize that all feelings are part of you, and you don't need to avoid any of them. You accept your feelings without labeling them good or bad, healthy or unhealthy. Noticing and accepting your feelings is also a major part of self-acceptance.

Physical Balance

Physical balance requires you to be mindful and respectful of your body. It includes being aware of the connection between your body and your mind, and paying attention to the messages your body sends to your brain. You can learn how to evaluate the state of your body continually, without becoming preoccupied or obsessed with it. How are you feeling physically? Are you tired, hungry, or thirsty? If you are experiencing discomfort or pain, where is it coming from and how bad is it?

Some common characteristics of a balanced physical experience are: stretching and exercising regularly, paying attention to your diet by eating healthy foods, maintaining your nutrition by taking vitamins as appropriate, avoiding toxins as much as possible, breathing intentionally, practicing relaxation, and getting enough sleep.

EXERCISE

When people are tired mentally and/or physically or in pain, they usually feel inclined to remain sedentary and avoid exercise; however, exercise is one of the best ways to promote physical balance. Physical movement is essential to health and well-being. Moving physically is a lubricant for your body, keeping it in the condition needed for daily activities. The danger of inactivity is that your body becomes de-conditioned, which can make it harder to engage in physical activity and add substantially to your perception and experience of pain.

Scientific studies have shown that regular and sustained physical activity is beneficial to virtually every system in the body. During exercise your body releases chemicals called endorphins, which naturally help to lessen anxiety and depression, as well as relieve pain.

Other benefits of regular exercise include:

- **Helping you maintain a healthy weight.** Dropping extra pounds helps reduce risks for a variety of health-related problems. It makes physical activity easier and more comfortable, in part by lessening the stress placed on your joints.

- **Increasing flexibility.** As your body gains flexibility, you can move more easily and are less likely to strain muscles and joints.

- **Helping you build strength.** The stronger you are, the better your muscles can take the load off joints and bones. The healthier the muscle, the less pain you feel.

- **Increasing serotonin level.** Serotonin is a neurotransmitter that improves mood, fights pain by blocking the perception of pain in the brain, and helps regulate sleep.

- **Protecting and strengthening the heart and circulatory system.** Exercise helps decrease the risk of stroke, heart attack, and diabetes. It also reduces high blood pressure.

- **Increasing dopamine levels, which result in improved moods and increased energy.** Regular exercise can boost your levels of dopamine, another critical neurotransmitter involved in regulating emotional responses, physical movement, and the brain's reward and pleasure center. Chronic drug use frequently depletes the brain's dopamine inventory.

The three major types of exercise are cardiovascular, strength training, and stretching. What is most important is to identify and participate in whatever forms of exercise best fit your individual needs and capacity.

Cardiovascular exercise—also known as aerobic exercise, and commonly referred to as "cardio"—is any type of exercise that increases the work of the heart and lungs. Walking, jogging, running, swimming, elliptical cross training, biking, climbing stairs, and rowing are common forms of cardiovascular exercise. The specific benefits of regular cardio include: improved heart function, reduced risk of heart disease, improved blood cholesterol and triglyceride levels, reduced risk of osteoporosis, and improved muscle mass.

Strength training is also called resistance training because it involves strengthening and toning your muscles by contracting them against a resisting force. There are two types of resistance training: **Isometric resistance** involves contracting your muscles against a non-moving object, such as against the floor in a push-up. **Isotonic strength training** involves contracting your muscles through a range of motion, as in weight lifting.

Strength training boosts metabolism, helps prevent and even reverse bone and muscle loss due to aging, and helps improve balance and coordination. By increasing balance and coordination, strength training can significantly reduce the risk of falling, a crucial benefit, especially as you get older.

Strength training doesn't require lifting weights, expensive machines, or a gym membership. Push-ups, squats, and lunges are examples of strength training exercises that require no equipment.

Stretching exercises are used to help keep the body—specifically muscles and ligaments—limber and flexible. Stretching can ease stiffness, increase your range of movement, reduce stress on joints, and increase the flow of blood and nutrients throughout the body. Stretching, or flexibility training, is a way to reduce injuries and increase joint mobility.

As you age, your muscles begin to tighten, lessening your range of motion. You find it's more difficult to do what you once found easy, such as picking up something from the floor, reaching for something over your head, turning your head while making a U-turn, or even getting dressed in the morning. Stretching helps lengthen your muscles and makes these everyday tasks easier.

Exercise is also an effective and healthy way to release energy and intense emotion. **Before beginning any exercise program, you should consult with your doctor or medical provider to be sure the exercises are appropriate and helpful for your specific situation.**

Describe your current involvement in exercise activities (cardio, strength training, and stretching). What activities do you participate in, and how frequently?

_____

_____

_____

If you do not currently participate in any exercise activities (remember, walking is a form of exercise) what do you need to do to start?

_____

_____

_____

What forms of exercise can you begin *now,* as a way of moving toward better physical balance and overall health?

_____

_____

_____

DIET AND NUTRITION

> Most people aren't as conscientious as they should be about getting all the daily nutrients they need.

What we eat every day has a profound effect on how we feel, how we cope with stressful life events, and how well we maintain our immune systems. Our diets play a major role in our health and well-being. A healthy diet with an emphasis on fruits, vegetables, and whole grains and proper nutrition can improve our well-being, help us fight many chronic diseases, and extend our lives. Foods high in saturated fats, like red meats, and refined sugar, like white bread, cause us to produce more insulin. More insulin means less fat breakdown, as well as a bigger appetite, which leads to overeating. As surely as certain foods, like those high in sugar and saturated fat, can make us more susceptible to disease, many foods can make us feel more energized, mentally alert, and keep us healthy. Some foods—those rich in fiber and those that are not processed—actually cleanse the digestive system, ridding the body of toxins that would otherwise build up in the bloodstream and spread throughout the body.

Most people aren't as conscientious as they should be about getting all the daily nutrients they need. However, improving the quality of your diet isn't as complicated as it might seem. The following strategies can help you change your diet for the better and improve your nutrition to enhance your physical balance and overall health:

- **Try to eat a balanced mix of foods** from the basic food groups: grains, vegetables, fruits, oils, milk, meat, and beans.

- **Think moderation.** It is not necessary to deprive yourself of the foods you love, even if they aren't the healthiest. Instead, limit foods containing more added sugars and solid fats and make sure the majority of the foods you eat are healthy.

- **Eat the right number of servings for you.** You can personalize the number of servings you need from each food group according to your age, gender, weight, height, and physical activity level with the USDA's MyPyramid Plan. This is an easy way to find out how much of each food group you should eat daily.

- **Eat foods that decrease inflammation.** According to the latest research, inflammation is one of the leading causes of disease in humans. To reduce inflammation significantly, reduce saturated and trans-fats, eat lots of green leafy vegetables, drink green tea, and consume Omega-3 fatty acids. The best sources of Omega-3 are those with high amounts of EPA and DHA like wild salmon, sardines, tuna, flaxseed, and walnuts. Another option is to take fish oil/Omega-3 supplements.

- **Include foods that boost immunity.** Studies on populations throughout the world have shown that foods can heal, and diets that prevent disease are typically high in whole grains, fruits, and vegetables and low in meats and saturated fats. Foods that are thought to be especially healthy include apples, beans, broccoli, cabbage, carrots, cauliflower, fish, garlic, grapes, nuts, onions, peppers, spinach, oranges, and tomatoes.

- **Limit processed foods.** Try to stay away from foods that have lengthy ingredients labels, especially when you can't pronounce or have never heard of some of the ingredients.

- **Minimize "white" foods**—white bread, white pasta, and white rice, and instead select more whole-grain foods—whole wheat breads and pasta and brown rice, which are naturally higher in nutrients and contain more fiber.

- **Be mindful of your consumption of sugar.** Recent evidence has made it clear that sugar is linked to a number of diseases such as diabetes, heart disease, hypertension, and cancer. Until a few years ago, the main dietary ingredient to avoid was fat. But as fat was replaced with sugar in many products, the incidence of heart disease went up, not down. Since this change, the average weight of the population has also gone up. We now know that the simple sugars found in soda and other sugary drinks, cookies, and candies, are also found in foods we might not even realize contain sugars. These are one of the main causes of the skyrocketing rates of obesity and Type 2 diabetes in the US.

> When it comes to diet and nutrition, focus on making gradual changes.
> You don't have to overhaul your diet all at once.

Supplementing your diet with select vitamins and minerals can help you achieve and maintain good nutrition. Vitamins are organic compounds required in tiny amounts to maintain bodily functions and fuel chemical reactions. Minerals are naturally occurring substances that are critical in physiological mechanisms such as bone growth, blood formation, muscle contraction, nerve conduction, and heart rate. The foods we eat are usually the best sources of vitamins and minerals. Unfortunately, we don't always eat the right foods, and the stress we're under may require more nutrients than we're getting. Keep in mind that it is always best to consult with your doctor or other medical provider when considering which vitamins and minerals to take and in what quantities.

When it comes to diet and nutrition, focus on making gradual changes. You don't have to overhaul your diet all at once. According to the US Department of Agriculture (USDA) Center for Nutrition Policy and Promotion, taking small, gradual steps over time to improve your diet and lifestyle can make a substantial positive difference in your overall health.

Describe your current dietary and nutritional routine.

_____

_____

_____

What changes in terms of eating a balanced mix of foods can you begin *now* to improve the quality of your diet and nutrition?

_____

_____

_____

What changes in terms of thinking in moderation and eating the right number of servings (for you) can you begin *now* to improve the quality of your diet and nutrition?

_____

_____

_____

What changes in terms of eating foods that decrease inflammation can you begin *now* to improve the quality of your diet and nutrition?

_____

_____

_____

What changes in terms of eating foods that boost immunity can you begin *now* to improve the quality of your diet and nutrition?

_____

_____

_____

What changes in terms of your consumption of processed and "white" foods can you begin *now* to improve the quality of your diet and nutrition?

_____

_____

_____

What changes in terms of your consumption of sugar can you begin *now* to improve the quality of your diet and nutrition?

_____

_____

_____

_____

SLEEP

Sleep is as important to health, well-being, and recovery as are air, food, and water. Sleep aids in the restoration of the central nervous system, conservation of energy, and information processing. Without enough sleep you are more likely to be anxious and irritable and have difficulty paying attention and concentrating. You become more susceptible to getting sick and your quality of life and health is diminished. Going without sleep for too long can cause psychosis and even death.

The amount of sleep required varies by individual and depends on many factors, and sleep needs change as a person grows older. Recommended sleep ranges from about nine hours a day for teenagers to seven to eight hours in adulthood. Some people sleep more; some sleep less. In middle age, sleep becomes lighter and nighttime awakenings become more frequent and last longer. For older persons, falling asleep tends to take longer and there are often multiple awakenings during the night. Despite the awakenings, over a twenty-four hour period older adults generally accumulate the same amount of total sleep as young people because they are more likely to nap during the day.

Sleep disorders are also closely associated with withdrawal, detoxification, post-acute withdrawal, and early recovery.

Sleep problems always complicate the treatment and recovery processes, making it more likely that people will leave treatment prematurely and against medical advice, as well as increasing the potential for relapse. It is helpful to keep in mind that long-term alcohol and other drug use has serious negative effects on the sleep cycle, and it will take some time for the effects of post-acute withdrawal to subside allowing for more and better sleep.

The most common sleep disorder is insomnia—difficulty falling asleep or maintaining sleep. Insomnia results in daytime fatigue and compromised reasoning, judgment, and mood. Insomnia is classified according to the part of the sleep cycle most affected: sleep initiation (falling asleep), sleep maintenance (frequent awakenings), or early awakening (terminal insomnia). Some people suffer with sleep apnea, which is a serious condition and should be referred to a competent medical provider.

The bottom line is that if people don't get a good night's sleep, they feel tired, anxious, and irritable, and have difficulty thinking clearly and concentrating. The consequences of ongoing sleep deficits include:

- marked decreases in mental performance,

- the inability to accomplish many daily tasks,

- reduction in motor functioning with a increased risk of accidents,

- mood disturbances, such as sadness, depression, and anxiety, and

- interpersonal difficulties where people get ornery and moody and have problems with family, friends, and coworkers.

Not getting a good night's sleep can be a challenge for anyone, but for someone in recovery, especially early recovery, it can be a real obstacle.

If you are experiencing insomnia or other sleep problems, before considering the option of sleep medications (which create a dependency on them to fall and stay asleep, making it that more difficult to sleep without them), it's important to do a thorough inventory with regard to your sleep habits or "sleep hygiene."

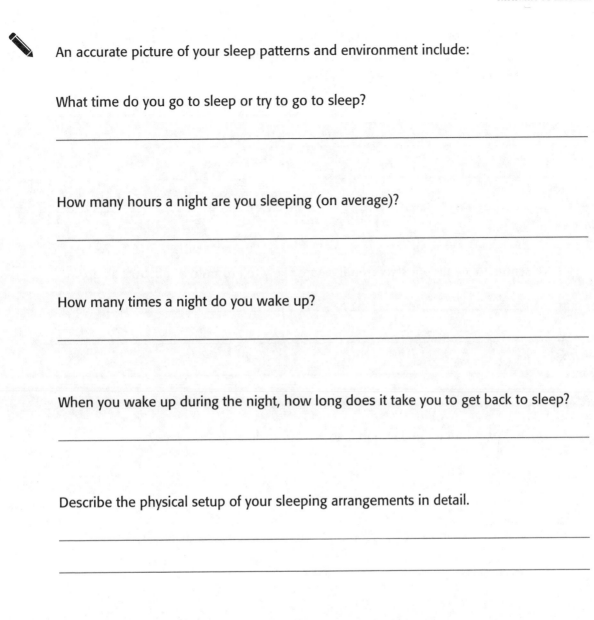

An accurate picture of your sleep patterns and environment include:

What time do you go to sleep or try to go to sleep?

_____

How many hours a night are you sleeping (on average)?

_____

How many times a night do you wake up?

_____

When you wake up during the night, how long does it take you to get back to sleep?

_____

Describe the physical setup of your sleeping arrangements in detail.

_____

_____

How conducive to healthy sleep are those arrangements for you? Be specific.

_____

_____

Describe your pre-sleep routines. What do you do prior to going to sleep? If you were watching yourself on a video screen during the last thirty to sixty minutes before you go to bed, what would you see (be specific)?

_____

_____

_____

_____

Describe how your pre-sleep routines are likely to promote or obstruct sleep.

_____

_____

_____

Do you nap during the day, and if so, for approximately how long?

_____

How much caffeine and/or nicotine do you consume on a daily basis?

_____

What time(s) of day/night do you consume caffeine and/or nicotine?

_____

_____

Not surprising, many people struggling with sleep problems in treatment and early recovery continue to consume caffeine via coffee, soda, and energy drinks, as well as smoke cigarettes or use electronic cigarettes. If you are among them, it's understandable that you may want to hold on to caffeine and nicotine since you're working to give up alcohol and other drugs. However, caffeine and nicotine are both stimulants that can interfere with sleep.

A healthy sleep routine includes:

- Paring down or discontinuing nicotine and caffeine—or at least avoiding caffeine after lunch and especially in the evening.

- Avoiding naps.

- Having a consistent pre-sleep routine that may initially require going to bed only when sleepy.

- Going to bed at about the same time each night.

- Turning off electronic devices, such as television and cell phones (white noise machines that reduce ambient sound and/or facilitate relaxation are an exception).

- Using the bed only for sleeping and sex.

- If unable to sleep, getting up and moving to another room—returning to bed only when sleepy.

- Getting up at about the same time every morning.

It's helpful for this routine to be as consistent as possible. This is especially true for people who are trying to develop healthy sleep habits.

You cannot force yourself to sleep, but you can create a physical, mental, emotional, and spiritual environment that is conducive to and sets the stage for sleep. It's helpful to minimize internal and external stimulation. Your bedroom/sleep space needs to be appropriately darkened. Putting a big, brightly lit digital clock in the bedroom where it is easily visible is unhelpful because most people will be drawn to looking at it and obsessing over the time that passes while they are getting to sleep. It pays dividends to force yourself to wake up at the same time, even when you have had trouble sleeping at night. This way you will be more tired and ready for sleep come nighttime (as long as you don't nap during the day).

Certain colors are more energizing and other colors more calming. Sleep comes more easily and is better in a cool room, literally, when the temperature is lower. That doesn't mean the person sleeping has to be cold; they can be warm under the covers, but the room temperature is on the cool side. If the person gets up during the night to use the bathroom, it's best to use minimal light. Turning on the bathroom light can start the brain thinking that it's daytime. For people living in places where there is a large amount of noise outside from traffic or whatever, a "white noise" machine can help to drown out the other sounds.

Exercise is critical to good overall health, but it can also greatly benefit one's quantity and quality of sleep. Physically active adults sleep more soundly than their sedentary, non-exercising peers. Clients can be guided to address their worries by writing them down before bedtime, and they can also plan for the next day by writing down what they need to do before bedtime.

Relaxation is an effective way to prepare the body and mind for sleep. Engage in any activities you find relaxing shortly before bed or while in bed. Listening to a relaxation or guided imagery recording, focusing on pleasant images, playing soothing music, meditating, or doing deep breathing or progressive muscle relaxation exercises can be helpful.

Describe three changes you can begin to make *now* to improve your sleep hygiene and give yourself opportunities to sleep better.

1. _____

_____

2. _____

_____

3. _____

_____

INTENTIONAL BREATHING

Proper breathing is one of the master keys to good health. It is also a connection to all of the Four Points of Balance. An important component of mindful self-awareness, intentional, conscious focus on breathing can achieve remarkable results, such as reducing stress, lowering blood pressure, improving digestion, increasing blood circulation, decreasing anxiety, and improving sleep and energy cycles.

> Proper breathing is one of the master keys to good health. It is also a connection to all of the Four Points of Balance.

How is it that intentional breathing—sometimes referred to as breathwork—can have such a powerful effect on one's health?

Unlike any other function of the body, breathing is the only one we do both voluntarily and involuntarily. As such, it is the only function through which we can access and influence the autonomic (involuntary) nervous system, which regulates the heart, circulation, digestion, and other vital functions. Imbalances in the autonomic nervous system are the root cause of many ailments, including hypertension, chronic stress, and disorders of circulation and digestion, to name a few.

Breathing Basics

Keep in mind the benefits of intentional breathing depend on daily practice and develop gradually and cumulatively. At first you will need to train yourself to engage in these techniques consciously, but with regular practice they can become a natural part of the way you breathe.

- **Observe your breath.** Whether you are only beginning or are an experienced practitioner, the most subtle and powerful form of breath work is also the simplest: Follow your breath. Sit or lie with your spine straight, close your eyes, and focus your attention on your breathing, without trying to influence it. Notice that following your breath as it comes in on your inhale and goes out on your exhale is pleasant and relaxing. It's a way of putting your mind and body in neutral. If your mind starts to wander, gently bring it back to your breathing.

- **Make your breathing deeper, slower, and quieter.** The more you can move your breathing in these directions, the more efficient your respiration will be—the more oxygen will be delivered to organs and the more harmoniously your nervous system will function. Whenever you think about it, whether stopped at a red light or waiting in a supermarket line, practice taking a series of breaths in which you consciously try to make your breath slower, deeper, quieter, and more regular. Taking slow, deep breaths is also a handy stress-reduction technique. If you pay attention to your breathing when you are angry, anxious, or otherwise upset, you will notice that your breathing is generally rapid, shallow, and irregular. Inevitably, these two conditions— distressing emotions and unconscious breathing patterns go together. Conversely, it's nearly impossible to be upset if your breathing is slow, deep, quiet, and regular.

- **Breathe abdominally.** Another way to use your respiratory system fully is to breathe abdominally through your stomach rather than your chest. When you inhale and take a breath in, focus on expanding your belly rather than your chest. An easy way to tell if you are doing this properly is to hold your hand over your abdomen as you take a breath. When you inhale, your hand should move outward, and when you exhale it should move back in. Whenever possible, pay attention to whether your belly is expanding and contracting as you breathe. Breathing through your stomach will help your breathing become deeper, slower, and quieter.

- **Exhale/squeeze out more air.** It is important to keep in mind that you deepen your breathing primarily by exhaling more air, not inhaling more. If you can push more air out of your lungs, your lungs will automatically take more in. Try taking a deep breath, letting it out effortlessly, and then intentionally squeezing more air out of your lungs. You should feel the effort in your intercostal muscles between your ribs. These are muscles that most people are not accustomed to using. If you do this exercise whenever you think of it, even at odd moments during the day, you will gradually build up these muscles, and your exhalations will become deeper. Through practice over time, the length of your exhalations will increase until they naturally equal that of your inhalations (in most people, inhalation lasts much longer).

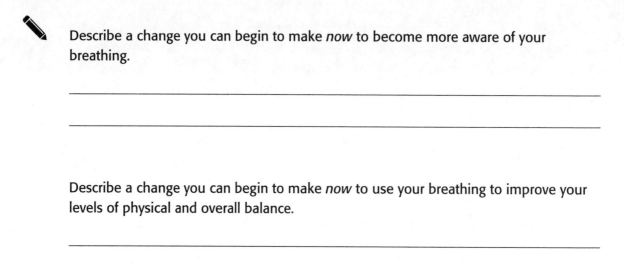

Describe a change you can begin to make *now* to become more aware of your breathing.

_____

_____

Describe a change you can begin to make *now* to use your breathing to improve your levels of physical and overall balance.

_____

_____

RELAXATION

Relaxation exercises generally combine breathing and focused attention to calm the mind and the body. There are a wide variety of relaxation exercises that you can learn to activate your body's "relaxation response." The relaxation response is the opposite of the "fight-or-flight" reaction that prepares your body for rapid action in response to perceived threats. The relaxation response helps to reduce and even reverse the physical, mental, and emotional effects of stress. Activating the relaxation response helps to facilitate the experience of that all-important but often elusive quality in recovery: serenity/inner peace/peace of mind.

Ongoing stress makes you more susceptible to illness and disease. It saps your energy and contributes to fatigue, negative thinking, and distressing emotions, including: anxiety, fear, frustration, anger, self-pity, and depression. According to medical research, stress is responsible for as much as 90 percent of all illnesses and diseases—most notably hypertension, heart disease, and cancer. In addition, stress can be a contributing factor in making existing medical conditions worse. Ongoing/chronic stress interferes with your attitude, social and family relationships, work, health, and of course, recovery. As a result, learning and practicing ways to relax in order to counteract the stress you experience is vital to health, balance, and recovery.

> Activating the relaxation response helps to facilitate the experience of that all-important but often elusive quality in recovery: serenity/inner peace/peace of mind.

Relaxation practices work by inducing physiological changes in the part of the central nervous system known as the **autonomic nervous system** (ANS), and specifically, the **parasympathetic division** of the ANS. The ANS regulates many organs and muscles, and it affects functions such as heartbeat, breathing, digestion, and sweating. The **sympathetic division** of the ANS triggers the "fight-or-flight response," which increases heart rate, breathing, and blood flow whenever we're stressed. The **parasympathetic division** of the ANS does the opposite by decreasing heart rate and breathing, reducing blood pressure, and causing us to slow down and relax. Practicing relaxation techniques reduces activity in the sympathetic division and increases activity in the parasympathetic division—stress and anxiety are reduced, heart rate is decreased, blood pressure is lowered, immunity is enhanced, energy levels are boosted, and physical balance is improved.

There are a variety of relaxation techniques that can stimulate your relaxation response and induce the experience of greater calm, including but certainly not limited to meditation (which will be discussed in the section on Spiritual Balance), progressive muscle relaxation, yoga, and Chi Kung.

PROGRESSIVE MUSCLE RELAXATION

Progressive muscle relaxation is an effective and time-efficient exercise that is an especially good fit for beginners and those who are action-oriented. It is a more physically "active" relaxation technique compared to others that are more passive, such as meditation or guided imagery. It is extremely helpful for people who have difficulty sitting still to access a more calm and relaxed state. Another benefit of progressive muscle relaxation is that it is easy to learn and practice.

Central Nervous System (CNS): Brain and spinal cord.

Autonomic Nervous System (ANS): Regulates activities of visceral muscles: heart, blood vessels, intestines, and glands.

Sympathetic Division:
Linked with arousal response and use of energy.

In reaction to perceived threats, prepares body for fight or flight by increasing blood pressure and heart rate, slowing digestion, and dilating pupils.

Parasympathetic Division:
Linked to conservation of energy, feelings of calm and relaxation.

Heart rate and breathing decrease, blood flow to skeletal muscles decreases, blood sugar levels fall.

Active in rest, relaxation, and digestion.

The basic idea behind progressive muscle relaxation is that tension is incompatible with relaxation. We are either in one state or the other, but we cannot be both tense and relaxed at the same time. In this exercise you consciously tense and then release specific muscle groups—this provides the opportunity to notice and experience the differences between when you are physically tight and when you are relaxed.

Sometimes we are aware of being tense, but often stress and muscle tension sneak up on us unconsciously. If you spend much of your time in a state of tension, you may have little idea what relaxed muscles are supposed to feel like.

To begin this process, sit or place yourself in a comfortable position:

- You can keep your eyes open or close them, depending on your preference.

- As you go through the various muscle groups in the order listed in the table below, tensing and relaxing them, tune into your breathing, taking full, deep breaths through your abdomen, and notice the sense of calm that accompanies the entire process.

- Let the stresses and tensions of the day dissolve and flow from your body.

- Allow yourself to let go of all your tightness and enjoy the warmth and the sensations of heaviness or lightness (you may experience either) as relaxation spreads throughout your entire body.

- Notice the profound difference between your tension and relaxation at each point in the process.

> If you spend much of your time in a state of tension, you may have little idea what relaxed muscles are supposed to feel like.

You may at times notice distracting or intrusive thoughts during progressive muscle relaxation (or any other relaxation exercise):

- There is no need to "fight" or avoid the thoughts (e.g., talking to yourself in ways like "Damn it, why can't I stop thinking about that?").

- Rather, refocus on your breathing as your breath goes out on your exhale and in on your inhale. You can also silently repeat a calming word or phrase like "relax" or "calm."

The actual exercise is as follows:

Go through each of the muscle groups listed below.

Tense/tighten each muscle group.

Hold that tension for about five seconds.

Then release the tension, allowing your muscles to become loose and relaxed.

Notice the dramatic differences between the sensations of tension and relaxation.

A word of caution here: do not tighten your muscles to the point where you feel significant discomfort or pain. The intent is to tighten and tense your muscles so you can experience a clear contrast between the sensations of muscle tension and relaxation. It is important to be especially careful when tensing your neck and your back. Be kind, caring, and gentle with yourself as you go through the process of becoming more relaxed.

PART OF THE BODY	TENSING METHOD
Hands and Fingers	• Clench your fists tightly. • Hold for five seconds. • Relax.
Forearms	• Extend your arms out against an invisible wall and push against it hard. • Hold for five seconds. • Relax.
Upper Arms	• Bend your elbows toward the floor, and tense your biceps. • Hold for five seconds. • Relax.
Forehead	• Wrinkle your forehead and lift your eyebrows as high as you possibly can (try to make your eyebrows touch your hairline). • Hold for five seconds. • Relax.
Central Face	• Turn your face into a hard grimace, squint your eyes, wrinkle your nose, and purse your lips. • Hold for five seconds. • Relax.
Lower Face and Jaw	• Clench your jaw hard. Draw the corners of your mouth back and grimace. • ALTERNATE METHOD: Open your mouth as wide as possible, as if you are silently screaming. • Hold for five seconds. • Relax.
Neck and Throat	• Press your head as far back as it can comfortably go. • ALTERNATE METHOD: Press your chin against your chest as far as it can comfortably go. • Hold for five seconds. • Relax.
Upper Back	• Pull your shoulder blades together, as if you were trying to get them to touch each other. • Hold for five seconds. • Relax.

PART OF THE BODY	TENSING METHOD
Shoulders	• Pull your shoulders up as if you were trying to touch your ears. • Hold for five seconds. • Relax.
Lower Back	• Arch and tighten your back. • Hold for five seconds. • Relax.
Abdomen	• Tighten and pull your stomach muscles in. • Hold for five seconds. • Relax.
Buttocks and Hips	• Pull in your buttocks, tightening these muscles as much as you can. • Hold for five seconds. • Relax.
Legs: Thighs, Calves, and Feet	• Tense your muscles in your legs by flexing your thigh and calf muscles and pulling your toes upward and toward your body. • Hold for five seconds. • Relax.

Having gone through the entire progressive muscle relaxation protocol, allow yourself to be fully aware of the difference between how relaxed you feel now compared to how you felt before doing this exercise.

YOGA

Yoga is a Sanskrit word meaning "union." Yoga is a discipline that can be traced back as far as 5,000 years ago. It was developed in India and promotes physical balance, health, and well-being by connecting the mind, body, and spirit together.

Those suffering with addiction often yearn for ways to release pent-up energies, fill a psychic hole, or relieve emotional pain trapped inside them. Yoga is an ideal modality to help address the physical aspects of recovery. People in recovery need to release toxins that have been stored in their bodies over the years. They need to release pain and trauma trapped in their muscles and joints.

> Yoga is an ideal modality to help address the physical aspects of recovery.

Throughout the centuries several distinct forms of yoga have emerged, although they all ultimately lead to the same place. Yoga practice has many forms and styles—there is a yoga tradition and exertion level that can fit the needs and capacity of almost every person. Among the best-known schools of yoga is **hatha** yoga, which emphasizes physical and breathing exercises.

Some more active styles of yoga include **integral** yoga, which aims to integrate the various aspects of the body and mind through a combination of postures, breathing techniques, deep relaxation, and meditation, where function is given preeminence over form; and **somatic** yoga, which is an integrated approach to the harmonious development of body and mind based on traditional yoga principles and modern psycho-physiological research. There are two forms of yoga that are especially slow-paced and gentle: **Viniyoga** focuses on slow stretches and deep breathing. This approach often is used to treat back and arthritis pain, and **Iyengar** yoga another gentle style that focuses on precise body alignment. Different props, such as straps, blocks, and blankets, are used in Iyengar yoga.

Yoga helps to increase mobility and reduce pain by stretching and strengthening the body. It is far more than a physical activity; it moves one mindfully into the body, breath, and consciousness of movement. The recovery- and health-related benefits of yoga include:

- **Stress reduction.** By encouraging relaxation, yoga helps lower the levels of the stress hormone cortisol. Related benefits include lowering blood pressure and heart rate, improving digestion, and boosting the immune system, as well as easing symptoms of conditions such as anxiety, depression, fatigue, asthma, and insomnia.

- **Healthier breathing.** Yoga teaches people to take slower, deeper breaths. This helps to improve lung function, trigger the body's relaxation response, and increase the amount of oxygen available to the body.

- **Greater flexibility.** Improving flexibility and mobility and increasing range of movement will reduce a person's aches and pains. Yoga helps improve body alignment, resulting in better posture and helping to relieve back, neck, joint, and muscle problems.

- **Increased strength.** Yoga postures use every muscle in the body, helping to increase strength. They also help relieve muscle tension.

- **Decreased pain.** Studies have shown that practicing yoga postures or asanas can help reduce pain for people with any number of conditions. Practitioners also report that emotional pain can be eased through the practice of yoga.

- **Weight management.** Yoga can aid in weight control efforts by reducing cortisol levels, as well as by burning excess calories and reducing stress. Yoga encourages healthy eating habits and provides a sense of well-being and self-esteem.

- **Improved circulation.** Yoga helps improve circulation and moves more oxygenated blood to the body's cells.

- **Cardiovascular conditioning.** Even gentle yoga practices can provide cardiovascular benefits by lowering resting heart rate, increasing endurance, and improving oxygen uptake during exercise.

- **Improved present-centeredness.** Yoga helps practitioners to focus on the present, to become more aware, and to create better mind-body health. It improves concentration, coordination, reaction time, and memory.

- **Serenity/inner peace.** The meditative aspects of yoga help many reach a deeper, more spiritual, and more satisfying place in their lives.

> For more information on yoga and recovery, I recommend *Yoga and the Twelve-Step Path* by Kyczy Hawk, Central Recovery Press, 2012, Las Vegas, NV.

CHI KUNG

Another discipline that helps move people in recovery toward balance is Chi Kung (sometimes spelled Qi Gong). Chi Kung is an ancient Chinese healthcare practice that integrates physical postures, breathing techniques, and focused attention. These three attributes make it an excellent complementary practice for anyone recovering from addiction and its physical, mental, emotional, and spiritual manifestations.

Like yoga, Chi Kung creates an awareness of and influences dimensions of our being that are not part of traditional exercise programs by combining the importance of mindful intent and breathing techniques in physical movements. Chi Kung is a precursor to Tai Chi though it has no martial arts applications. It utilizes the life-force energy known as "chi" in eastern medicine and involves the body's meridian system (also used in acupuncture). There are few lifestyles that do more to deplete and dissipate our chi than active addiction. Chi Kung restores and balances chi.

> Chi Kung is an ancient Chinese healthcare practice that integrates physical postures, breathing techniques, and focused attention.

Chi Kung is moving meditation and is an especially gentle form of exercise. Its gentle, rhythmic movements help to reduce stress, promote relaxation, improve posture, increase flexibility and range of motion, reduce pain, build stamina, increase vitality, and enhance the immune system. Chi Kung has also been found to help improve breathing and lung capacity and lower blood pressure, as well as strengthen cardiovascular, circulatory, lymphatic, and digestive functions. Consistent practice helps one regain vitality, maintain health during aging, and speed up recovery from illness. One of the more important long-term effects of Chi Kung is that it reinforces the mind-body-spirit connection.

Specific exercises help practitioners release negative energy and focus on specific areas of the body such as the spine. For beginners, the exercises known as the "Eight Section Brocade" are particularly valuable.

Eight refers to the number of individual exercises in the form that when practiced together impart an energetic quality in the body that is analogous to a piece of richly woven cloth (hence, "brocade"). It is an easy-to-learn, time-tested, safe system of Chi Kung. Chi Kung is a comprehensive program that allows students to pace themselves as they move from level to level within the discipline.

> For more information on Chi Kung and recovery, I recommend *Chi Kung in Recovery* by Gregory S. Pergament, Central Recovery Press, 2013, Las Vegas, NV.

Make sure to check with your doctor or other healthcare provider before beginning any type of exercise program, including yoga or Chi Kung.

Additionally, it's important to let your yoga or Chi Kung instructor know of any specific physical problems or challenges you may have. It is never helpful to push yourself too hard too fast, exceed your capabilities, and injure yourself. That being said, pushing yourself to go beyond your comfort zone is part of the process of learning and growth.

✎ Write a list of balancing physical activities you can look into and begin to practice.

_____

_____

_____

_____

Spiritual Balance

Spiritual balance involves cultivating an awareness of a connection between self, others, and that which is beyond oneself—God/Nature/the Universe/Spirit/the Divine, etc. It is about taking care of oneself and being of service to others. Whatever life brings, those who are spiritually balanced are able to find ways to deal with it, knowing that even though the situation may not be okay, they will be okay. Spiritual balance helps people find meaning and purpose, even in situations that are uncomfortable and painful.

Spirituality refers to the area of life concerned with matters of the spirit, those aspects of life beyond oneself. It includes a sense of connection with others, and to the world around you—an experience of being part of a greater whole. Spirituality emphasizes the commonalities all people share that link us together. It provides an antidote for the experience of feeling different and disconnected from others and from the world.

> Spiritual balance helps people find meaning and purpose, even in situations that are uncomfortable and painful.

When talking about spirituality, it is important to note this discussion does not refer to religion. However, spirituality does not preclude religion. For some people, spirituality is closely connected to organized religion and a belief in God. For others, spirituality has absolutely nothing to do with organized religion and/or a belief in God. You can be an atheist and still live a deeply spiritual life. You do not have to believe in a God to live a principle-centered life based on values, beliefs, and ethics you embrace. The process of recovery allows you the freedom to choose what form your spirituality will take based on the right fit for you.

In active addiction you can become so beaten down that you become hopeless. The majority of your thoughts center on various forms of doom and gloom, and your relationship to others and the world is increasingly negative.

Active addiction collapses the world, making it much smaller as life revolves around using and finding the ways and means to continue to use. Spirituality expands the world, helping you reconnect with that which is greater than yourself and move toward becoming the person you are meant to be.

As twelve-step programs have demonstrated over many decades with millions of people, developing a sense of spirituality—in the form of coming to believe in a power greater than oneself and learning and practicing certain spiritual principles such as acceptance, tolerance, patience, compassion, humility, and faith—is an essential part of the process of recovery.

Feeling confused or ambivalent about spirituality is understandable. The most important aspect of developing spirituality is being honest about your feelings, where you are at in your life, and what your beliefs are, along with how these beliefs manifest in your perspective, attitude, and behavior. Your challenge here is to be open to the possibility that growing a relationship with a power greater than yourself is a dynamic key to learning how to cope with life in ways that are balanced, healthy, and helpful.

The most important aspect of developing spirituality is being honest about your feelings, where you are at in your life, and what your beliefs are, along with how these beliefs manifest in your perspective, attitude, and behavior.

What does spirituality mean to you?

_____

_____

_____

_____

_____

Describe your current spirituality.

_____

_____

_____

_____

_____

There are many practices that can contribute to and enhance spiritual balance. These include, but are certainly not limited to, prayer, staying in the moment/mindfulness, meditation, and gratitude.

PRAYER

Spiritual traditions around the world incorporate myriad forms of prayer. Many people maintain a belief in the healing power of prayer. Regardless of whether you use prayers based on an established religion or from the literature of a twelve-step program or you have come up with your own form(s) of prayer, the act of communication with a higher power is the intention.

Prayer is basically a spiritual process of asking for help. You may have some familiarity with "foxhole" prayers, so-called because of the expression, "There are no atheists in foxholes." These are prayers, or more accurately pleas, to God (or whoever/whatever) to fix some urgent problem or to help you avoid the potential consequences of some horrible situation you got yourself into. Usually this type of prayer involves promising that if your prayers are answered, you'll do anything—never use again, entirely change your life, etc.

You may have the impulse to pray for a specific outcome, but the process of prayer is much bigger than that. Praying for solutions to specific problems is usually a setup for disappointment. Some people use prayer to ask for help in their practice of spiritual principles, for example, to have greater open-mindedness, courage, emotional strength, compassion, humility, and/or faith. Some use prayer to express gratitude for whatever blessings they have. Others may pray for patience in waiting for the outcome of a situation and acceptance of that outcome, whatever it may be. Still others ask for help in finding the best and highest purpose for the day ahead.

Prayer can take many different forms. Sometimes it is formal and other times it is informal. Your process of prayer may include specific rituals or consist of simple communication in a conversational manner with your higher power. Prayer may be done in solitude, or in communion with and in the company of others. People adopt a wide variety of different body postures for prayer such as kneeling, standing, or sitting. Your practice of prayer will evolve as your understanding of recovery continues to grow and your needs change.

Describe your experience with prayer.

_____

_____

_____

If you use prayer in your recovery process, describe your practice of it (be specific about when and how you pray).

_____

_____

_____

_____

If you do not yet use prayer as part of your recovery process, how might you begin to use it (be specific about when and how)?

_____

_____

_____

_____

STAYING IN THE MOMENT

A number of approaches to spirituality emphasize the value of staying in the moment, that is, being present-centered in this moment, right here and right now, as opposed to focusing on what has already happened in the past or could potentially happen in the future. Recovery, and indeed life, occurs one day at a time. But actually, they happen one moment at a time. Life unfolds in this exact moment, right here and right now.

Unfortunately, most people are caught up in thinking about what happened in the past (a minute ago, an hour ago, yesterday, last week, two months ago, last year) or what may happen in the future (in a few minutes, an hour from now, tomorrow, next week, next month, etc.). This is so common and so normal that we don't even realize it's happening; it occurs automatically and unconsciously. Thoughts about what has happened or might happen pop into our heads and we run with them, often to mental and emotional places that have nothing to do with this moment.

Everyone has a past, and it's okay and even healthy to visit it from time to time in order to better understand it, put it in perspective, and to learn from it. And obviously, looking at and planning for the future is important and positive. It's when so much time is spent in the past or the future that your conscious focus is distracted from the here and now that it becomes problematic. Besides, you can neither change the past nor predict or control the future. The only aspect of time and experience you have influence over is this moment—right here and right now.

There are many ways in which staying in the moment promotes health, healing, and recovery. In being present-centered and living just for today, you make yourself genuinely physically, mentally, emotionally, and spiritually available to see the possibilities inherent in this moment and the opportunities for learning and growth that it presents. Mindfulness and the related practice of meditation are among the most helpful techniques to stay in the moment.

MINDFULNESS

Mindfulness is the practice of paying conscious attention to the present moment by tuning in to one's internal and external experience. Mindfulness creates a receptive state in which one observes and accepts his or her thoughts and feelings as they are, without judging them. Mindfulness cultivates the ability to witness one's own experience without becoming over-identified with or attached to the content of thoughts, emotions, and physical sensations *or* trying to avoid or suppress them.

This is especially relevant for people in recovery in that mindfulness can bring about the skill of observing cravings to use and urges to avoid or suppress pain, and ride them out, rather than act on them reflexively and unconsciously. By facilitating conscious awareness with a detached nonjudgmental perspective, mindfulness decreases the tendency to get caught up in vicious circles of anxiety, fear, anger, guilt, regret, and shame that render those in recovery from addiction more vulnerable to relapse.

Mindfulness helps people learn to relate to discomfort—whether that discomfort is physical, mental, or emotional—differently. When an uncomfortable feeling like a craving or anxiety arises, people who practice mindfulness are better able to recognize their discomfort and observe it with presence and compassion, instead of automatically reaching for a drug to make it go away.

> Mindfulness creates a receptive state in which one observes and accepts his or her thoughts and feelings as they are, without judging them.

The practice of mindfulness stimulates the understanding that thoughts and feelings, including urges to escape, numb, and avoid by using, are always temporary. Through mindfulness and meditation, it is possible to learn how to face uncomfortable, painful thoughts, feelings, and physical sensations—learning simply to accept the pain, anxiety, anger, or sadness and let it pass—without obsessing on or needing to change it, potentially by using. Research has demonstrated that the practice of mindfulness meditation leads to improvements in attention, concentration, openness to experiences, ability to inhibit distracting stimuli, and perceptual sensitivity.

MEDITATION

Meditation is one of the main ways of achieving a state of mindfulness. For many people, it is an important part of the recovery process. **Meditation** quiets the mind helping to still the ongoing thought-based chatter in our heads, giving us greater opportunity to tune in to the present moment. For people in recovery, practicing meditation is highly recommended. The Eleventh Step in twelve-step programs focuses on using prayer and meditation to build and strengthen a relationship with a higher power of one's own understanding. In this context, prayer is often thought of as a way to *talk to* one's source of spirituality, while meditation is a way to *listen to* that source of spirituality.

> Meditation quiets the mind helping to still the ongoing thought-based chatter in our heads, giving us greater opportunity to tune in to the present moment.

Meditation connects the mind and body and facilitates balance by counteracting stress, activating the parasympathetic division of the autonomic nervous system and stimulating the relaxation response. Practicing meditation reduces activity in the sympathetic division, which triggers the fight-or-flight response, and increases activity in the parasympathetic division.

One of the main reasons meditation has been around for over 2,500 years is that it's extremely simple. Ironically, because life can be so complicated for so many people (especially those in recovery), its simplicity can make it even more challenging. The purpose of meditation is to set aside the distractions that constantly clamor for your time and attention, and consciously slow down and quiet your mind, starting with your thoughts, to bring you to this moment, here and now.

A common question asked by people beginning meditation is "How do I stop my thoughts?" The answer is you don't. The desire to "stop" thoughts mobilizes both resistance and judgment, which work against meditation's fundamental intent. Even during meditation, other thoughts, including those related to the past or future, naturally intrude. This intrusion is neither positive nor negative; it simply is. After all, your thoughts don't stop simply because you are meditating.

When your mind wanders (and it will), the most helpful thing you can do is to become aware of the thoughts and simply notice and observe them, without judging either the thoughts or yourself for having them. They can float by like clouds overhead. There is no need to be disturbed by them, obsess over them, or try to change them. You become aware that you have drifted away from the moment, and use that awareness to matter-of-factly refocus your attention and come back to the here and now.

There are many ways to meditate and it's important to find an approach that fits for you. One form of meditation is based directly on mindfulness. This approach centers conscious attention on internal and external sensations using a relaxed though focused observation of thoughts, emotions, and bodily sensations as they arise and fall. Breathing meditation focuses on the breath—being consciously aware of your breathing, making that the locus of attention as you slowly and deeply breathe in on your inhale and out on your exhale. Mantra meditation concentrates conscious attention on a mantra, an energy-based sound that produces a specific physical vibration, and may or may not have any particular meaning. The word mantra means "to free yourself from your mind."

There are also guided meditations available on digital formats where your attention follows the voice suggestions on a recording to help you access meditative states.

Find a quiet space. Meditation is most effective (particularly for beginners) when there are minimal distractions. And since focused attention is the most basic element of meditation, as much as you can, ensure wherever you choose to meditate is quiet and peaceful for the duration of the exercise.

Assume a comfortable position because muscle tension can disrupt your attention and interfere with relaxation; physical comfort is important. You can use any position, but the most effective is a sitting position in a chair or on a firm pillow or rug, with your head, neck, and back straight. Lying down to meditate is generally not recommended as many people have a tendency to become too drowsy and fall asleep.

Be aware that when you first start to meditate, it may seem strange and awkward, especially if it is difficult for you to be still both mentally and physically. It's often best to begin slowly, perhaps with three to five minutes a day and gradually work your way up to fifteen to twenty minutes.

When breathing, close your mouth, place your tongue loosely on the roof of your mouth, and breathe smoothly through your nose. Follow the "Breathing Basics" detailed in the section on Intentional Breathing, breathing deeply and slowly through your stomach rather than your chest and exhale completely before the next inhale.

Consistency is key; if at all possible, try to meditate at the same time of day and in the same location. In this way, you develop a pattern and rhythm for your meditation practice that will help establish it as one of your "habits of recovery." Morning works well for many people because it sets a tone for the day; for others evening is a better fit because it helps them wind down. What's most important is to meditate regularly, even when you may not feel like it or think you don't have time for it. Five minutes of meditation is much better than nothing.

The health benefits of meditation and mindfulness practice are wide-ranging and have been documented by scientific research for over thirty years. Although the benefits of meditation and mindfulness practice start almost immediately—stress and anxiety are reduced, heart rate is decreased, blood pressure is lowered, immunity is enhanced, and energy levels are boosted—the positive effects are also cumulative over time. Recent research using functional magnetic resonance imaging (fMRI) finds that meditation produces positive changes in the brain's ability to process emotions that endure even when people are not actively meditating.

In addition to decreasing stress, with all of the secondary health gains that come with that, meditation has a protective impact on heart health by contributing to measurable decreases in cardiac risk factors. Empirical studies have demonstrated that meditation practice can help reduce high cholesterol; reduce insulin resistance, glucose, and even insulin levels; reduce blood pressure and hypertension; and reduce the risk of heart disease and stroke among individuals over the age of fifty-five.

Meditation practice enriches the brain, enhancing connections between neurons. When you exercise parts of the brain, which occurs during meditation, they become larger and denser with neural mass or gray matter. Studies also indicate meditation has neuroprotective effects, mitigating some of the impacts of aging in the brain. The volume of the brain's gray matter ordinarily diminishes with age. However, scientists found that in meditators (in contrast to a comparison group of nonmeditators), the volume of gray matter hadn't decreased with age.

Moreover, meditation can help people face physical pain more successfully. Research has shown that meditation can reduce both the experience of pain and pain-related brain activation. Meditation expands the ability to consciously change how pain is perceived, and better accept the pain that is experienced, without obsessing over or trying to change it.

Describe your experience with meditation.

_____

_____

_____

If meditation is part of your recovery process, describe your practice of it.

_____

_____

_____

If you do not yet use meditation as part of your recovery process, how might you begin to use it (be specific about when and how)?

_____

_____

_____

GRATITUDE

Another important part of the recovery process related to spiritual balance is cultivating an attitude of gratitude for whatever blessings you have. There are no guarantees of anything and we can take nothing for granted in this life. Every day is a gift; every breath is a gift. Gratitude changes perspective; it can sweep away most of the petty, day-to-day annoyances that so many of us focus on, such as the "small stuff" experiences that bring up feelings of impatience, intolerance, negative judgment, indignation, anger, or resentment.

> Gratitude changes perspective...

Sometimes you may have to look a little harder to see the blessings in your life, but there is always something to be grateful for, no matter how negative or desperate the situation seems. You can learn, perhaps to your surprise, that it is possible to remain in conscious contact with gratitude in spite of feelings of anxiety, sadness, anger, depression, fear, or physical pain.

Gratitude is an emotion expressing appreciation for all you've received, all that you have, and for all that has not befallen you. It is the opposite of being discontented that you don't have what you want or have what you don't want. Over the past decade, numerous scientific studies have documented the mental, emotional, social, and physical benefits of gratitude. These benefits are available to most anyone who practices gratitude, even in the midst of adversity, such as elderly people confronting death, women with breast cancer, and people coping with chronic disease. This would seem to easily apply to anyone in recovery from addiction. Research-based reasons for practicing gratitude include:

- **Gratitude brings us happiness.** Practicing gratitude is one of the most reliable methods for increasing happiness and life satisfaction. It also boosts feelings of optimism, joy, pleasure, enthusiasm, and other positive emotions. On the flip side, gratitude reduces anxiety and depression.

- **Gratitude promotes physical health.** Studies suggest gratitude lowers blood pressure, strengthens the immune system, reduces symptoms of illness, and makes one less bothered by aches and pains.

- **Gratitude enhances sleep.** Grateful people tend to get more hours of sleep each night, spend less time awake before falling asleep, and feel more rested upon awakening. If you want to sleep more soundly, count blessings, not sheep.

- **Gratitude increases resiliency.** It has been found to help people recover from traumatic events.

- **Gratitude strengthens relationships.** It makes one feel closer and more connected to friends and intimate partners. When partners feel and express gratitude for each other, they each become more satisfied with their relationship.

- **Gratitude encourages "paying it forward."** Grateful people are generally more helpful, generous of spirit, and compassionate.

By intentionally cultivating gratitude, you can increase your well-being and strengthen your recovery. Being grateful is a skill that can be developed with practice. Two specific ways you can practice gratitude are by making "gratitude lists" and writing "gratitude letters." A gratitude list consists of writing down three to five things for which you're grateful every day or, at minimum, every week. A gratitude letter is one you write to someone in your life to express appreciation for ways he or she has helped you and/or been there for you. Gratitude letters can be about events that have happened in the past or are happening in the present. Gratitude letters often help to strengthen or repair relationships.

SPIRITUAL PRINCIPLES

Learning and practicing various spiritual principles is also an extremely valuable component of spiritual balance and the overall process of recovery. Spiritual principles represent values and ethical standards. They form a suggested code of conduct by which to live. The practice of spiritual principles is emphasized in twelve-step programs of recovery. However, such principles are universal—they have been part of most of the world's important spiritual traditions for centuries.

> Spiritual principles represent values and ethical standards. They form a suggested code of conduct by which to live.

There are many different spiritual principles, one of which is gratitude. A handful of others are described below. Some of these may seem so straightforward that you may not have considered them spiritual principles. Yet, that is precisely what they are. They represent the complete opposite of how people usually conduct themselves in active addiction. Applying these principles in your life will strengthen your recovery and help you become more whole, healthy, and healed.

Acceptance

Acceptance means to recognize, acknowledge, and come to terms with the reality of a given situation or fact. It is important to understand that accepting something does not imply one agrees with or is happy with it. You can dislike situations and still accept them. Finding ways to accept those things that are beyond your control to change provides freedom from having to fight against the realities you find uncomfortable/painful.

Open-Mindedness

Open-mindedness means being respectful of and receptive to new and different possibilities. This includes being open to suggestions and ideas that you haven't previously considered and perspectives and beliefs that may be significantly different from your own.

Responsibility

Responsibility means to be dependable, conscientious, and reliable. It's about doing the work necessary to fulfill one's obligations and follow through on commitments—whether these relate to others or to oneself.

Honesty

Honesty is the spiritual principle that calls for sincerity and truth telling with oneself as well as with others. It is an essential aspect of working a program of recovery and involves striving to extinguish both overt dishonesty (lies of commission/telling untruths) and covert dishonesty (lies of omission/withholding the truth).

Integrity

Integrity is when what you do is consistent with what you say—when your actions match your words. It also reflects that how you seem on the outside fits with how you feel on the inside.

Courage

Courage is the spiritual principle of remaining steadfast and undeterred through challenges or adversity. It involves persevering through one's fear in order to accomplish a goal. Accepting responsibility for certain of your actions requires courage. Practicing courage does not mean not having fear, it means you can be afraid and still do whatever it is you need to do. Courage is risk-taking for your betterment. In active addiction you likely took large-scale risks, maybe even placing yourself or people you care about in dangerous circumstances. Recovery requires the courage to take healthy risks, such as trusting others, allowing yourself to feel and share your emotions, talking and writing about painful parts of your past, and making significant life changes.

Humility

Humility is acknowledging and accepting one's own assets and liabilities/strengths and weaknesses based upon a realistic view of oneself. Like all human beings, you are neither all good nor all bad. In practicing the spiritual principle of humility, you also acknowledge that you need the assistance of others and a connection to that which is beyond yourself in order to recover.

Patience

Patience is the ability to wait without worry or complaint. Another form of patience is allowing time to pass before responding, making a decision, or taking action. It includes being tolerant with and of others. Allowing another person the space to experience and express his or her feelings is a powerful demonstration of patience. When a person is actively applying the spiritual principle of patience, he or she does not react in frustration or anger when something does not turn out as desired.

Faith

Faith is belief that is not based on actual evidence/proof. The practice of faith includes the belief in a power beyond yourself, along with a conscious relationship with that higher power. In addition to courage, it takes faith to walk through anything you fear, and the greatest faith comes from walking through those circumstances you are most afraid of. Living in faith means trusting that situations will work out the way they need to (which may well be different from the way you want them to) and that you will be okay.

Forgiveness

To forgive is to let go of ill will, resentments, or grudges that you have toward other people, groups, or institutions. Forgiveness can be extended to others whether or not they admit their part in a conflict or other situation. When you hold on to ill will and resentments you hurt yourself much more than any one else. When you get caught up in resentment, you become attached to the source of that resentment—giving them power over you as the intense emotions eat away at you like acid, and the thoughts that drive those emotions consume space in your head, stealing your time and attention. Forgiving is not about approving or condoning what someone has done, it's about letting go of it. It's helpful to keep in mind that forgiving oneself can be a part of the process of learning to forgive others.

Service

Service means to help or assist others. It is about making positive contributions to one's environment, often in the form of giving back or paying forward. Service is usually associated with volunteering one's time and energy—this can be on a one-time or situation-specific basis, or an ongoing commitment. Service can take many different forms. People can be of service to their families, friends, community organizations, neighborhoods, etc. Being of service is an important part of twelve-step program participation, where the intent is to give to others in the same way that others have given to us.

Self-acceptance

Forgiving oneself for our past misdeeds is also part of self-acceptance. Self-acceptance is being okay with oneself without reservation. It is the sense that you are "good enough," exactly as you are, with all of your challenges and areas in which you seek to improve. It is the understanding and knowledge that nobody, including you, has to be perfect in order to belong in this world.

The more you can remain in conscious contact with these spiritual principles—and practice prayer, staying in the moment/mindfulness, meditation, and gratitude—the more spiritual balance you will have. The more spiritual balance you have, the better equipped you will be to cope successfully and skillfully with the full range of experiences that life will present you with. When you build a balanced foundation of spirituality you maximize both your internal harmony and the potential for harmony between yourself and others.

Describe at least three things you can begin to do *now* to improve your spiritual balance.

_____

_____

_____

_____

_____

_____

Describe *how* you will begin to do those things (be specific).

_____

_____

_____

_____

_____

_____

The balancing effects of enhanced spirituality and its positive impact on your recovery may become apparent only gradually over time. It can be weeks or even months after these processes first begin before you realize that your awareness, thoughts, feelings, and behavior have started to change.

The Value of Twelve-Step Program Participation

Twelve-step programs are the most successful and widely available resource for individuals seeking recovery from addiction. Twelve-step programs use a mutual-support approach to recovery from addictive and other compulsive behaviors, based on a set of guiding principles. The Twelve Steps were originally developed in 1935 by the fellowship of Alcoholics Anonymous (AA) to help people recover from alcoholism.

After AA, the next twelve-step program to evolve was Narcotics Anonymous (NA). NA was established in 1953 to apply the twelve-step approach to recovery from all mind- and mood-altering substances. NA does not distinguish between different drugs of abuse, including alcohol, and focuses on recovery from the disease of addiction. Research demonstrates that practicing the Twelve Steps has a profound and positive impact on life functioning, as well as the ability to maintain abstinence from substances.

> Twelve-step programs are the most successful and widely available resource for individuals seeking recovery from addiction.

Because it has been so successful, the twelve-step model expanded to include programs that focus on specific drugs—Cocaine Anonymous (CA), Crystal Meth Anonymous (CMA), Heroin Anonymous (HA), and Pills Anonymous (PA), or specific types of behavior—Gamblers Anonymous (GA), Sex Addicts Anonymous (SAA), Overeaters Anonymous (OA), and Codependency Anonymous (CODA), to name a few.

Auxiliary twelve-step programs such as Al-Anon and Nar-Anon—for friends, partners, and family members of those struggling with addiction—came about in response to the understanding that addiction affects everyone close to it, and is often enabled by well-meaning significant others. These programs have helped many millions of people worldwide to recover from addiction in all of its various manifestations.

Research shows that a combination of professional addiction treatment and participation in twelve-step programs is often the most effective route to recovery. However, professionally provided treatment always has an endpoint. Inpatient and residential treatment, while providing care twenty-four/seven, usually lasts from mere weeks to a few months (occasionally residential programs last a year), and access to it depends on individual financial resources, adequate health insurance coverage, or modest publicly funded services. Intensive outpatient treatment consists of combinations of individual, group, and family counseling for ten to twenty hours per week, usually for up to six months. Non-intensive outpatient treatment has the longest duration (up to a year or sometimes more), but only provides between one and three hours per week of individual and perhaps group counseling.

While treatment is of a limited duration, recovery is a never-ending process. Twelve-step program participation can last as long as people desire. Many people maintain ongoing, even lifelong involvement in twelve-step programs as a way to continue their learning, growing, and healing. Unlike counselors and other treatment professionals, in many communities NA and AA meetings are available throughout the day and evening, seven days a week, 365 days a year.

NA and AA focus on the need for continuous abstinence from mind- and mood-altering substances and are based on behavioral, cognitive, and spiritual principles and practices that help people learn how to stay in recovery one day at a time.

These principles and practices are contained in the Twelve Steps and include:

- Accepting powerlessness over the fact of one's addiction.

- Acknowledging that willpower alone cannot achieve sustained recovery.

- Connecting to others who have been through similar experiences is essential to combat isolation and provide social support and mutual aid.

- Having faith in a power beyond oneself, providing an antidote for the fear and self-centeredness of active addiction.

- Letting go of the need to try to control people and situations.

- Examining past errors with the help of a sponsor (an experienced member who serves as a mentor).

- Making amends for those errors.

- Recovery involves a process of spiritual renewal that uses the tools of meditation, prayer, and applying spiritual principles; and being of service by helping others who want to achieve recovery.

As effective as the twelve-step programs of recovery have proven to be—more people have achieved and maintained recovery from addiction through twelve-step programs than any other method, by far—they aren't perfect. They have their critics, and you may encounter unhelpful individuals or aspects of twelve-step recovery that rub you the wrong way. If you look for reasons to complain or not participate, you will find them—the same as in any other area of life.

It is not uncommon for people to find attending twelve-step meetings uncomfortable, at first. You are encouraged to check out different meetings in order to find those that are the best fit for you. New experiences are often uncomfortable and adjusting to them usually takes some time.

For some, the focus on spirituality in twelve-step programs can be a turn-off. As described in the section on Spiritual Balance, spirituality is a fundamental part of life and health. It's important to keep in mind that twelve-step programs are spiritual, not religious. For some twelve-step program members, spirituality and religion are connected; for many members they are not. There are atheists who have been in recovery for decades in twelve-step programs. The twelve-step process of recovery allows you the freedom to choose what form your spirituality will take, based on the right fit for you.

> It is not uncommon for people to find attending twelve-step meetings uncomfortable, at first.

Much of the language and philosophy of twelve-step recovery can be strange and perplexing to the newcomer. The suggestion to "take what you need and leave the rest," in most cases, means to embrace what makes sense to you in early recovery and set the rest aside. You may come back to it with greater understanding when you have more time and experience in recovery.

For people seeking recovery, twelve-step programs provide a widely available and remarkably effective support system by surrounding them with people who have gone through and are going through the same struggles. Having access to the knowledge and experience of others who have remained abstinent and have built successful recovery for themselves is an invaluable source of support, hope, and encouragement.

As explained earlier, people in recovery need to separate from many of their previous friends (the people in the "people, places, and things") associated with using. It can be a big challenge for recovering addicts to learn to build relationships without the assistance of alcohol and other drugs. Twelve-step programs provide the opportunity to develop new and healthier relationships, build new friendships based on significant shared values and goals, and help you learn how to have fun without using.

Twelve-step programs create an environment that promotes emotional safety, where people have the experience of being connected and feeling understood and accepted unconditionally. For people recovering from addiction who so often feel so different—many of whom struggle with anxiety, fear, sadness, depression, guilt, shame, and loneliness—this is an incredibly big deal.

There are many individual differences among the people at any given twelve-step meeting, including all the colors of the racial and ethnic rainbow and the entire socioeconomic spectrum: from service workers and blue-collar tradespeople to physicians, attorneys, and other white-collar folks, to those who are homeless and desperately indigent. Addiction is a powerful equalizer, and a shared interest in recovery brings together an extraordinary assortment of people who may look different on the outside but have many of the same thoughts and feelings on the inside.

What people did during active addiction—to themselves, to loved ones, and to others—and the depths to which they sank en route to finding the motivation to attempt a new approach to life and the goals they share in recovery—the desire to remain free from active addiction and learn how to live a meaningful and value-directed life—can generate a connection that translates to deep mutual understanding, acceptance, and support in recovery.

Make no mistake about it: recovery is hard work. Achieving and maintaining recovery takes dedication and persistence. A drive-by or every-once-in-a-while approach won't get it done. In order to be successful in recovery, a person genuinely has to want it and be willing to make the effort. But then, maintaining active addiction also requires plenty of work. Practicing addicts typically devote multiple hours each day to feeding their active addiction—planning and pursuing the ways and means to use, using, recovering from the acute effects of using, and starting the cycle over again.

> Achieving and maintaining recovery takes dedication and persistence.

Most people give little thought to the tremendous amount of time and energy it takes to support their addiction; they simply do what they have to do. Yet, many of these same individuals express concern about the amount of time and energy maintaining recovery requires. Quite a few of them are ultimately unwilling to invest much time and energy in dramatically changing their lives for the better.

Anyone willing to put anywhere near the same amount of time and energy into his or her recovery that he or she gave to active addiction will be successful in recovery. However, even if you are willing to give only 25–50 percent of the time, attention, and energy to recovery that you previously spent chasing your active addiction, you will have excellent opportunities to be successful. What you do with those opportunities is up to you.

NOTES

_____

_____

_____

_____

_____

_____

TRAUMA, ADDICTION, AND RECOVERY

There is an important connection between addiction and trauma. People who have had traumatic experiences are more likely to use alcohol and other drugs as a means of coping with their trauma and may become addicted. People who are addicted to alcohol and other drugs are more likely to put themselves in situations where they are at greater risk of experiencing trauma.

Having trauma can complicate the process of recovery from addiction. This section is designed to improve your awareness of trauma and its many forms and effects, and how trauma and addiction often occur together to create special challenges, as well as enhance your ability to turn that awareness into action in support of your recovery. The bottom line is that what happened to you in the past does not have the final say in who you become.

Please note: If you experienced trauma, you may be struggling with upsetting emotions, frightening memories, or a sense of being unsafe that seem to follow you around. Or you may feel numb, disconnected, and have difficulty trusting other people. These are common reactions to trauma. In the event the material presented here brings up anxiety, fear, anger, grief, sadness, or other intense emotions that are difficult for you to handle, it is important for you to be aware of these reactions and talk about them with someone you can trust and feel safe with. You can distinguish between "there and then" and "here and now."

What Is Trauma?

Trauma is a mind-body reaction that occurs in response to events that involve death or the possibly of death, serious injury, or threats to one's physical and/or psychological security. **Trauma** is a Greek word meaning "wound." Trauma is the result of extraordinarily stressful events that disrupt a person's sense of safety and security, and lead to feelings of vulnerability and helplessness.

> Although traumatic experiences often involve a threat to life or safety, any situation that leaves you feeling overwhelmed and alone can be traumatic, even if it doesn't involve physical harm.

Traumatic events overwhelm an individual's ability to cope with the emotions, sensations, and other information connected with that experience. Trauma may involve a single brief event, an event that lasts for hours or days, a series of events, or a situation that is ongoing. The word "trauma" is often used as shorthand for both events and their impact because the actual experience of violence or disaster and the aftereffects on one's sense of self and safety are intertwined.

Although traumatic experiences often involve a threat to life or safety, any situation that leaves you feeling overwhelmed and alone can be traumatic, even if it doesn't involve physical harm. Traumatizing events can be directly experienced, witnessed, or even learned about from others or seen/read about in news reports. In general, the closer to the event someone is, the more traumatized he or she is likely to become. In other words, those who directly experience the event are more likely to be traumatized than those who witnessed or learned about it, and those who witnessed the event are more likely to be traumatized than those who learned about it indirectly. Moreover, the more severe an event is and the longer it lasts the more likely it is to be traumatizing.

Trauma can be especially harmful when it occurs during childhood because children are much more vulnerable and have much less capacity to understand and process their experiences. Childhood trauma results from anything that interferes with a child's sense of safety and security, including:

- An unstable or unsafe environment

- Extended or repeated separation from a parent/primary caregiver

- Serious illness or pain conditions

- Intrusive medical procedures

- Sexual, physical, or verbal abuse

- Domestic/intimate partner violence

- Neglect

- Bullying

It is not the objective facts about an event that determines whether it is or was traumatic, but rather your subjective emotional experience of that event. What is traumatic for you might not be for someone else and vice versa. How people respond to events varies considerably, and that response is influenced by multiple factors, including how the immediate environment responds—most importantly one's family and community. The more frightened, helpless, and alone you feel, the more likely you are to be traumatized. However, anyone can become traumatized.

Trauma changes the way people perceive the world. It changes how people process information and emotions and can cause lasting harm to people's emotional and social development by dramatically altering one's beliefs about safety, both physical and emotional. Trauma interferes with the ability to trust and feel safe. Sometimes the inability to feel safe is strongly and clearly felt, but it can also be more subtle. It can manifest as a feeling of numbness, as a vague sense of discomfort, or that something is "off."

> Trauma changes the way people perceive the world.

The Effects of Trauma

Research demonstrates that traumatic experiences change the brain and alter certain physiological or bodily responses. Beyond that, experiencing trauma changes one's life. Your behavior, your outlook on the future, your attitude and beliefs about people are all impacted by the experience of trauma. There is no "right" or "wrong" way to think or feel in response to trauma. Following a traumatic event, most people experience a wide range of emotional and physical reactions. Developing trauma symptoms is never a sign of weakness. **These are normal reactions to abnormal events.**

Physical Symptoms of Trauma	Emotional and Psychological Symptoms of Trauma
• Being startled easily • Hypervigilance (consistently being on guard) • Racing heartbeat • Aches and pains • Fatigue • Difficulty concentrating • Edginess and agitation • Muscle tension • Insomnia or nightmares	• Shock, denial, or disbelief • Feeling generally unsafe • Anger and irritability • Mood swings • Guilt, shame, or self-blame • Sadness, depression, feelings of hopelessness • Distressing memories or thoughts about the event(s) • Confusion, difficulty concentrating • Difficulty trusting • Anxiety and fear • Withdrawing from others • Feeling disconnected, detached, or numb

In the best-case scenario, trauma symptoms last from a few weeks to a few months and then gradually fade. But even when you're feeling better or "back to normal," these symptoms can reoccur. This typically happens in response to triggers, such as an anniversary of the event, images, sounds, smells, and situations that remind you of the traumatic experience. However, the effects of trauma can remain with survivors for much longer—often years, and sometimes decades—after the traumatic event(s).

Grieving is normal following trauma. Whether or not a traumatic event involves permanent injury or death, survivors must cope with the loss of their sense of safety and security, at least temporarily. Depending on the nature of the trauma, survivors also often experience the loss of whatever sense of innocence they had. The natural reaction to such loss is grief. Like people who have lost a loved one or gone through a divorce, trauma survivors go through a grieving process.

> Whether or not a traumatic event involves permanent injury or death, survivors must cope with the loss of their sense of safety and security, at least temporarily.

Trauma Can Take Many Forms

When we think of trauma what typically comes to mind are horrific events, such as war, acts of terrorism, natural disasters (hurricanes, tornadoes, forest fires, and earthquakes), plane or train crashes, motor vehicle accidents, or violent crime (public shootings, murders, and physical/sexual assaults). These are sometimes referred to as **"Big-T" traumas**. Big-T traumas are experiences with clear beginnings and end points.

Tragically, many people experience trauma within their own families. More obvious forms of trauma in the family include being subjected to and/or witnessing physical or sexual abuse. Yet, the majority of people experience a more subtle and chronic form of trauma. Sometimes known as **"small-t" traumas**, they come from repetitive experiences that usually occur during childhood and adolescence.

Small-t traumas can be any life experience that causes lasting harm to a person's sense of self and self-esteem. They often result from various forms of abandonment and rejection that children experience when their parents/primary caregivers are not physically or emotionally available in the ways those children need. Name-calling, put-downs, verbal abuse, living with the uncertainty of not knowing *if* or *when* a parent is coming home, or the fear that comes with listening to one's parents argue/fight night after night can be traumatic for any child. These traumas are common for people in recovery, especially those who grew up in addicted, violent, impoverished, or otherwise unstable or even unsafe family systems and neighborhoods where they experience them on an ongoing basis.

It's important to be aware that small-t traumas are not less significant than "bigger" traumas. The distinction is made to recognize trauma can be caused by seemingly smaller events that happen over an extended period of time.

Previously, these experiences were not viewed or treated as potentially traumatic.

However, because the events occur repeatedly, even if they continue to be upsetting and painful, the affected person (usually a child) becomes used to them. When such events are woven into one's ongoing life experience they don't stand out as being unusual; they become "normal" and just "the way it is."

The cumulative effect of these small-t traumas is substantial, but they may remain hidden from those who experience them. The thoughts and feelings endure, but they have not been emotionally processed and persist in the unconscious mind outside of conscious awareness. When a traumatized child becomes an adult and gets involved in relationships (both romantic and social) that bring up feelings connected to such past experiences, those traumas can be triggered. They lead to conflict or arguments that commonly involve over-the-top emotional reactions completely out of proportion to the current situation. Instead of responding consciously in the *here and now*, the person is reacting unconsciously from the *there and then*.

The vulnerability you experienced as a child—the pain, losses, distorted beliefs about yourself and how things were, and the ways in which you learned to protect yourself—all follow you into your adult life. These are trauma responses.

There is another form of trauma that deserves mention. **Intergenerational trauma** is trauma that is transmitted across generations and often occurs to groups of people. This is trauma that has been effectively transferred from a first generation of trauma survivors to the second and later generations of children of those survivors. This relates to the descendants of immediate victims of and witnesses to: genocide, slavery, racially/ethnically based violence and persecution, terrorism, totalitarian political regimes, and abuse in religious organizations. Descendants experience the victimization symptoms themselves, without the transfer of original trauma being recognized and help offered. Specific examples include, but are not limited to: Native Americans, Holocaust survivors, Japanese internment camp survivors, and African Americans. Domestic/intimate partner violence, sexual abuse, and extreme poverty are also sources of trauma that can be transferred to subsequent generations.

Looking in your past, identify any traumatic experiences you have been through. Remember, trauma can be a huge one-time event, a few big events, or more subtle ongoing experiences in one's family or community.

_____

_____

_____

_____

_____

If you've experienced trauma, describe any trauma symptoms you have experienced (review the lists on page 165).

Physical symptoms of trauma:

_____

_____

_____

_____

Emotional and psychological symptoms of trauma:

_____

_____

_____

_____

> The connection between trauma and addiction is a two-way street: trauma increases the risk of developing addiction and active addiction increases the likelihood of experiencing trauma.

The Connection between Trauma and Addiction

There is a clear relationship between trauma and addiction. Although addiction is not caused by trauma, and trauma is not caused by addiction, it has become increasingly clear that trauma and addiction frequently go together. Extensive research suggests that approximately 50 percent of people with histories of addiction have experienced trauma.

Based on different scientific studies, the percentage of people with both trauma and addiction ranges from about 20 percent to as high as 80 percent, with the figure being somewhat higher for women than for men. The connection between trauma and addiction is a two-way street: trauma increases the risk of developing addiction and active addiction increases the likelihood of experiencing trauma.

HOW TRAUMA INCREASES THE RISK OF DEVELOPING ADDICTION

People use alcohol and other drugs as a way to find temporary relief from the distressing effects of trauma. Using can be a form of self-medication to numb or escape intrusive memories, distressing thoughts, and painful emotions related to traumatic experiences. In this way, addiction may begin as a coping method and evolve into an emotional survival strategy.

When trauma-related memories or emotions surface and are too much to handle, many people seek the rapid relief available through using. When using provides the relief they're looking for, they gravitate toward it obsessively and compulsively, and over time and through repetition it becomes addiction.

Frequently, alcohol and other drug use increases in response to the surfacing or intensifying of trauma symptoms. Using allows trauma survivors to disconnect from their feelings—dampening shame and guilt, softening anger and rage, displacing anxiety and fear, and reducing sadness and depression. Depending on the particular substance(s), using can also serve other purposes for people with trauma helping them to increase feelings of relaxation, of being in control, or of simply feeling "alive."

Describe the relationship between your use of alcohol and other drugs and the trauma you've experienced (be specific).

_____

_____

_____

_____

HOW ACTIVE ADDICTION INCREASES THE LIKELIHOOD OF EXPERIENCING TRAUMA

The obsessive-compulsive cycle of using alcohol and other drugs impairs judgment and decision-making in ways that often lead to risk-taking behaviors and puts people in situations that greatly increase the likelihood they will be traumatized or (if they have been traumatized previously) re-traumatized. This trauma most often takes the form of physical assault/mugging, robbery, or sexual assault/rape. The need to find the ways and means to continue to use often results in risk-taking behaviors and puts people in situations that greatly increase the likelihood they will be traumatized or re-traumatized.

The urgency of avoiding the misery of withdrawal and becoming "sick" can lead to risk-taking behaviors. And, of course, being under the influence puts people at much greater risk of being traumatized or re-traumatized. Sometimes the resulting trauma involves the person under the influence who is traumatized, and sometimes his or her actions create trauma (including serious injury or death) for others.

Describe how your using put you in situations that increase your risk of being traumatized or re-traumatized (be specific).

_____

_____

_____

_____

CHILDHOOD TRAUMA AND ADDICTION

Research confirms that the more trauma you are exposed to the more vulnerable you become to developing addiction. As noted previously, trauma is particularly damaging when it occurs in childhood. Although some addicts have no apparent childhood trauma, it is estimated at least half have suffered one or more forms of severe childhood stress, and many have had multiple traumatic experiences.

Young children do not have a frame of reference to put traumatic experiences in context or to make sense of them. The primary source of support for children is the family, and yet the family is most often a source of trauma during childhood.

The *Adverse Childhood Experiences (ACE) Study*, which is based on data from over 17,000 Kaiser Permanente HMO members, found correlations between childhood trauma and various forms of addiction. The *ACE Study* is one of the largest scientific investigations ever conducted on the effects of childhood stress/maltreatment/trauma on health and well-being in adulthood. In the study, adverse childhood experiences were defined as follows:

- Recurrent and severe physical abuse

- Recurrent and severe emotional abuse

- Sexual abuse involving physical contact

Growing up in a household with:

- An addicted family member

- An incarcerated family member

- A mentally ill, chronically depressed, or institutionalized family member

- A mother who was treated violently

- Both biological parents not being present

The *ACE Study* found that adverse childhood experiences are much more common than most people think, although they are usually concealed from others outside the family and frequently go unrecognized. There is a direct correlation between the number of adverse childhood experiences (ACEs) someone has had and the number and severity of problems related to addiction, mental health, and physical health he or she experiences as an adult.

In other words, the more ACEs someone has, the more problems he or she will have as an adult and the more serious those problems will be. Specifically, a child with four or more of the above adverse childhood experiences is five times more likely to become an addict compared to children with no history of ACEs; a boy with four or more of these experiences is forty-six times more likely to become an injection drug user than other children. Trauma was also linked to a higher risk of anxiety disorders, depression, and suicide. The researchers also found that the effects of childhood trauma are cumulative, and that one of the most destructive forms is "chronic recurrent humiliation" (e.g., verbal/emotional abuse in the form of name-calling or ridicule).

Using the list on page 170, identify what, if any, adverse childhood experiences you went through.

_____

_____

_____

_____

_____

What's the Difference between Stress and Trauma?

As described in the section on Roadblocks to Recovery, **stress** is our natural automatic physiological response to perceived threats. It is what activates the flight or fight reactions that originally evolved in order to help our early human ancestors survive during times in history when actual threats to survival were constant. Stress served to mobilize the body in response to real physical dangers with the potential to kill—such as encountering a saber-toothed tiger or an unfamiliar and hostile tribe.

> …the body's stress response doesn't know the difference between physical and emotional threats or between dangers that are real and those that are imagined.

In response to stress, adrenaline (also known as epinephrine) and cortisol are released through biochemical reactions—increasing blood pressure and heart rate, making breathing faster and more shallow, elevating blood sugar, dilating pupils, and slowing digestion, all of which prepares the body for rapid action and provides energy. Stress activates the sympathetic division of the autonomic nervous system (part of the central nervous system), which triggers the "fight, flight, or freeze response."

As described earlier, the body's stress response doesn't know the difference between physical and emotional threats or between dangers that are real and those that are imagined. When you're stressed over a busy schedule; an argument with a friend, coworker, partner, or child; a traffic jam or your monthly bills, your body reacts essentially the same way as it would if you were facing a life-or-death situation.

Everyone experiences stress from time to time. It is normal and natural. However, not everyone experiences trauma. The difference between stress and trauma is similar to the difference between worrying and a feeling of real panic. Both are unpleasant and upsetting. But worry, like stress, is an unavoidable part of life, whereas panic, like trauma, can disable your thinking and severely interfere with your ability to function in your daily life.

Trauma is stress run amok. When stress activates the flight, fight, or freeze reaction, usually within hours or a few days, the nervous system calms down and returns to a normal state of equilibrium. When people are traumatized their nervous systems often remain stuck on high alert. Depending on the severity and complexity of the traumatic event(s), whatever had been normal may disappear altogether along with the memory of the event that caused the trauma.

A stressful event is most likely to be traumatic if:

- It happened unexpectedly
- You were unprepared for it
- You felt powerless to prevent it
- It involved intentional cruelty
- It happened in childhood
- It happened repeatedly

Describe any stressful events you've been through that you haven't previously thought of as being traumatic, but now looking back at them might have been traumatizing for you.

_____

_____

_____

_____

_____

Chronic, ongoing exposure to stress—regardless of whether or not you are in actual physical danger—is traumatizing. It has unhealthy effects on nearly every system in the body: raising blood pressure, suppressing the immune system, increasing the risk for heart attack and stroke, and even speeding up the overall aging process. Like other repetitive experiences, long-term stress rewires the brain, leaving people more vulnerable to fear, anxiety, depression and, of course, stress.

One way to begin to identify when stress has become traumatic is by looking at how much a stressful event affects your reactions, your relationships, and your overall functioning.

> Like other repetitive experiences, long-term stress rewires the brain, leaving people more vulnerable to fear, anxiety, depression and, of course, stress.

Trauma can be distinguished from stress by considering the following questions:

- How quickly is upset (anxiety/fear, sadness/depression, guilt/shame, frustration/anger/rage) triggered?

- How frequently is upset triggered?

- How intense is the upset?

- How long does the upset last?

- How long does it take to calm down?

How fast do you find yourself becoming anxious/fearful, sad/depressed, guilty/ashamed, or frustrated/angry/full of rage?

_____

_____

_____

How often do you find yourself becoming anxious/fearful, sad/depressed, guilty/ashamed, or frustrated/angry/full of rage?

_____

_____

_____

On a scale from 0 to 10 (where 0 represents experiencing none of these reactions and 10 represents the most intense experience of them) how would you rate your anxious/fearful, sad/depressed, guilty/ashamed, or frustrated/angry/full of rage reactions?

_____

_____

How long do your anxious/fearful, sad/depressed, guilty/ashamed, or frustrated/angry/full of rage reactions tend to last?

_____

_____

_____

After your anxious/fearful, sad/depressed, guilty/ashamed, or frustrated/angry/full of rage reactions run their course, how long does it take to calm down?

_____

_____

_____

The more quickly and frequently upset is triggered, the more intense and long-lasting the upset is, and the longer it takes to clam down, the more likely it is that trauma is involved.

What's the Difference between Trauma and Post-Traumatic Stress Disorder (PTSD)?

Most people will be exposed to a traumatic event at some point in their lives. With the passing of time, usually several weeks to several months, most people will process the event, the effects of trauma calm down, and gradually they heal and return to normal daily functioning. The trauma fades to a memory, painful but not problematic. While many people experience traumatic events, not everyone who experiences trauma develops post-traumatic stress disorder. PTSD occurs when the effects of trauma do not get better with time, and the mind and body effectively become stuck in a traumatized state. If the trauma is especially severe, prolonged, or life threatening, there can be long-term changes in the brain and the effects can be debilitating, interfering with their daily life on an ongoing basis.

> PTSD occurs when the effects of trauma do not get better with time, and the mind and body effectively become stuck in a traumatized state.

PTSD can create significant distress for both the person suffering from it and for those living with him or her. Typically, for those with PTSD, this distress impairs their social, occupational, or other important areas of functioning. PTSD is an actual mental health/psychiatric diagnosis defined by the presence of specific symptoms. These symptoms can be divided into four main categories:

1. Re-experiencing

2. Avoidance

3. Persistent negative changes in cognition (thinking) and mood (feeling)

4. Changes in arousal and reactivity

RE-EXPERIENCING

Re-experiencing symptoms involve reliving the traumatic event in various forms, including:

- Invasive memories of the trauma through thoughts, feelings, and images related to the event, which come up again and again and cause great distress.

- Nightmares connected to past trauma that recurs.

- Flashbacks—a vivid and powerful re-experiencing of the traumatic event as if it were happening in the here and now.

- Feelings of anxiety, fear, and high stress, when exposed to similar stimuli/situations that symbolize the traumatic event or remind the person of it.

Describe any re-experiencing symptoms you have experienced.

_____

_____

_____

_____

AVOIDANCE

Avoidance refers to those symptoms that involve distancing oneself from the trauma, disconnecting from others, and difficulty experiencing positive emotions. These symptoms include:

- Avoiding thoughts, emotions, and conversations connected to the trauma.

- Avoiding places, activities, and people that are reminders of the trauma.

- Forgetting significant parts of the traumatic event.

- Loss of interest in previously important and positive activities.

- Feeling distant and disconnected from other people.

- Feeling numb, along with difficulty feeling and expressing any emotion.

- Difficulty feeling and expressing positive emotions such as happiness, joy, or love.

- Lack of desire to think or talk about the future.

You may have extensive thoughts about what happened but feel no emotion. Or you might experience strong emotions but without thoughts or actual memories of the event(s). Sometimes people alternate between unable to remember all or parts of the trauma and vividly reliving it.

✎ Describe any avoidance and emotional numbing symptoms you have experienced.

_____

_____

_____

_____

_____

_____

PERSISTENT NEGATIVE CHANGES IN COGNITION (THINKING) AND MOOD (FEELING)

This area refers to symptoms that involve ongoing and distorted blame of oneself and/or others, along with a persistent negative emotional state.

These include:

- Persistent negative beliefs.

- Disproportionate or inappropriate assigning of blame or responsibility to oneself or other people.

- Feelings of alienation.

- Diminished interest in life.

✎ Describe any symptoms you have experienced in the area of persistent negative changes in cognition (thinking) and mood (feeling).

_____

_____

_____

_____

CHANGES IN AROUSAL AND REACTIVITY

Symptoms related to arousal and reactivity are the consequence of heightened anxiety and physiological tension. These symptoms include:

- Hypervigilence (constantly being on guard).

- Reckless, aggressive, or destructive behavior.

- Difficulty falling and/or staying asleep.

- Exaggerated startle reaction (jumpy/easily startled).

- Feelings of intense anxiety.

- Prone to irritability, overreacting, and/or unprovoked outbursts of anger.

- Difficulty concentrating.

- Reduced tolerance for pain.

Describe any symptoms you have experienced related to changes in arousal and reactivity.

_____

_____

_____

_____

_____

_____

Trauma and the Brain

The brain plays a central role in how we interpret and make sense of all of our experiences. Due to their overwhelming nature, traumatic events often can't be processed by the brain in the same way other experiences are processed. Trauma reactions often take on a life of their own, haunting survivors, as the effects continue to disrupt the normal flow of life—mentally, emotionally, physically, and spiritually.

> Due to their overwhelming nature, traumatic events often can't be processed by the brain in the same way other experiences are processed.

This section may seem technical and complicated, but it provides helpful information on how the brain works; how brain functioning affects our thinking, feeling, memories, and physical functioning; and how trauma affects the brain. In turn, this may help you better understand your own experiences with trauma.

The parts of the brain most affected by trauma are the neocortex and the limbic system. The **neocortex** is the most recently evolved and advanced part of the human brain. It gives us the abilities for abstract thinking, speech, moral reasoning, and delaying gratification, as well as the capacity to process past experiences to use what we have learned to inform our decisions in the present. The **limbic system** is considered the "emotional center" of the brain and is directly involved in emotion, memory, and motivation.

Ordinarily, there is ongoing communication between the neocortex and the limbic system as emotions and memories are connected with thinking and present experience. Trauma disrupts this communication. Trauma short-circuits the ability of the brain and nervous system to integrate traumatic experience and memories into conscious awareness and understanding. Traumatic memories are submerged in the limbic system—most notably the amygdala and hippocampus—where they are inaccessible to the thinking and reasoning parts of the brain (the neocortex) and operate unconsciously.

The **amygdala** is connected to motivation and arousal, as well as the formation and storage of emotional memories. It is active in the processing of emotions such as fear, anger, and pleasure, as well as the release of certain hormones. We are continuously and automatically taking in information from the environment around us. The amygdala interprets this information as to whether it is safe or there is danger. In this way, it functions as the brain's alarm system.

The **hippocampus** is involved in the formation of new memories and is also associated with learning and emotions. To form a specific memory, the hippocampus brings together information recalled from all aspects of an event and stores them as short-term memories. After a time and under "normal" conditions, the hippocampus reorganizes these memories and moves them into other parts of the brain. This converts short-term memories into long-term memories. Our personal database of information is built and expanded *gradually* as short-term memories are created and then converted into long-term memories that are stored away so we can retrieve them at a later time.

When we experience an event (any event), the amygdala signals the hippocampus to check the database of memories for past instances of this event or similar events. It integrates information from internal chemistry, external events, and memories, attaches the emotions, and decides an action.

The **hypothalamus** is linked to the limbic system. Known as the body's thermostat, the hypothalamus maintains **homeostasis,** the internal equilibrium or balanced state in which our body operates when healthy. This homeostasis includes the regulation of heart rate, blood pressure, body temperature, growth, metabolism, electrolyte balance, hunger, sleep, wakefulness, and breathing. The hypothalamus connects the brain with the endocrine system. The **endocrine system** consists of the glands that release hormones, which affect the action and functioning of various organs.

> The instinctual drive to survive takes over like an autopilot mechanism.

Trauma activates the amygdala, which determines that danger exists, and triggers the fight, flight, or freeze chemical response: *Do I run away, do I fight, or do I shut down?* "Whichever it is, I am going to do it right now." The instinctual drive to survive takes over like an autopilot mechanism.

Trauma freezes thinking. Usually our thoughts and feelings are closely connected. Trauma separates these from one another. It's as though the limbic system (where the amygdala and hippocampus are located) and the neocortex stop communicating with each other as the amygdala assumes control.

When you've been traumatized your amygdala becomes hypersensitive. It overreacts to normal stimuli. Our thought process depends on acquisition and retention of memories, but the process that builds memory is disrupted because the amygdala needs to focus its attention on the immediate potential danger. Basically, the brain determines there is no time for the hippocampus to store information in memory to use later because action must be taken right now.

In response to an event, which may have nothing whatsoever to do with the previously experienced trauma, when the amygdala asks the hippocampus to check for memories of this or similar events, the information that comes back is missing essential pieces. This faulty information distorts the emotions the amygdala attaches to what's happening in the present. That's why the emotions of someone who has experienced trauma can seem so disconnected from or out of proportion to events in the here and now.

When a child is traumatized, he or she may not remember the trauma, but this inability to remember the trauma can have different explanations. The memory may be kept unconscious (outside of his or her awareness) for self-protection because it is too painful, or the trauma may have occurred before the child had the capacity to create a memory of it. Although the amygdala is fully formed at birth, the hippocampus is not fully functional until about the age of four. When children are traumatized prior to the age of four they may not have a formed memory of it.

The autopilot response to danger (whether real or imagined) activated by trauma creates a cycle in which the hypothalamus sends nerve impulses to the pituitary and the adrenal glands, and the rest of the nervous system is stimulated to either trigger or inhibit responses from the rest of the body's organs, tissues, and glands.

The hypothalamus signals for the release of stress hormones adrenaline and cortisol that facilitate flight, fight, or freeze by raising blood sugar, blood pressure, and heart rate and shutting down digestion. The surge of adrenaline causes increases in heart rate, blood pressure, breathing rate, and metabolism. Cortisol facilitates the body's use of proteins, carbohydrates, and fats to provide rapid increased energy.

As noted earlier, this is a mechanism that evolved long ago in order to maximize the chances of survival, for both the individual and the human species. The brain assesses the presence of a threat and sends the signals that initiate the body's response to that threat. Because the perceived threat is immediate, the focus is on survival *right now*. We don't survive long-term if we don't successfully respond to danger in the present. Ideally, the stressful/traumatic circumstance that initiates the above chain reaction of automatic responses is short-lived and quickly resolved. If that happens, the brain has the opportunity to reset and our body returns to "normal" functioning.

Unfortunately, what is necessary for short-term survival works against long-term health. When trauma turns into post-traumatic stress, even long after the traumatic event(s) have passed, the brain doesn't reset and the body's resources are drained as they continue to be expended. The stress hormone cortisol continues to be released. An excess of cortisol leads to decreased production of white blood cells and antibodies. This excess depletes the immune system and makes people more vulnerable to illness and disease.

> Unfortunately, what is necessary for short-term survival
> works against long-term health.

The brain and body become stuck in "on-guard mode/hypervigilence," continuously sensing potential danger all around, constantly ready to flee, fight, or freeze. The traumatic event has passed but the person still suffers from trauma symptoms, unable to distinguish between danger and safety. So, if you've been traumatized and have had the experience of:

- feeling generally unsafe and being on-guard;

- having trouble managing your emotions, whether they seem out of control causing you to feel too much, or you are numb and feel too little;

- having difficulty remembering pieces of your past experience;

- feeling consistently uptight and stressed; then

- it is important for you to know there are very real brain-based reasons for it.

Retraumatization

People who have experienced trauma have a heightened vulnerability to other traumatic events. Once someone has been traumatized he or she is more susceptible to being retraumatized in the future. Similar to a physical wound, when someone experiences a traumatic event, he or she becomes susceptible to "rewounding" or retraumatization. Moreover, it appears that having previously experienced a traumatic event increases the likelihood of developing PTSD when exposed to another traumatic event.

> Once someone has been traumatized he or she is more susceptible to being retraumatized in the future.

The term **retraumatization** means to be traumatized *again*. It refers to experiencing another traumatic event and the impact(s) of that experience on you. Like trauma, retraumatization can be experienced directly or indirectly as a result of witnessing a traumatic event in person or on television or in a movie. For people who have been traumatized previously, even being close to someone who has experienced trauma and is having trauma reactions can cause retraumatization. Thus, retraumatization, like trauma, is transferable from one person to another.

Trauma Reenactment

As strange as it may seem, people who have been traumatized often place themselves in situations reminiscent of their original trauma. This is referred to as trauma reenactment. **Trauma reenactment** is a process of repeating patterns—related to circumstances, behavior, and people—connected to the traumatic event(s).

There are many vivid examples of this phenomenon. Children traumatized by the abandonment of a parent or the divorce of their parents frequently reenact these experiences in future relationships as adults. They may go through life with the belief they are destined to be abandoned and end up creating real-life situations in which that belief becomes a reality. They set themselves up for failure by gravitating toward romantic relationships and friendships in which they are likely to be rejected or abandoned.

Children who grow up in home environments with abuse and/or addiction often become involved in abusive or addictive relationships as adults. They may leave a relationship in which there is abuse and/or addiction, only to quickly become involved in another. This can happen repeatedly.

Women may be compulsively attracted to men who are practically or emotionally unavailable. Men may behave in ways that drive women away, as well as be drawn to women who are likely to leave them. Women sexually abused as children or teenagers may act in sexually provocative ways with others. Men emotionally abused by emotionally unavailable or distant mothers often end up in relationships with women who have similar traits.

Combat veterans frequently choose high-risk helping professions when they return from war. They also tend to pursue high-risk recreational activities that stimulate the adrenaline rush of their war-related experiences.

Why would anyone repeat such negative, painful experiences? It is important to remember this repetition does not occur on a conscious level. The person reenacting his or her trauma is almost never consciously aware that it is related to earlier life experiences. People are unconsciously driven to repeat these patterns because their trauma and related pain remains unprocessed and inadequately integrated in terms of conscious understanding and brain functioning.

Reenactments can occur for different reasons. Trauma survivors may be drawn to similar situations and relationships because of the comfort inherent in familiarity. In recreating the familiar, the repetitive aspect of trauma reenactment can provide the individual with a false sense of control and comfort, even if those reenactments are painful or dangerous for them. Reenactments can also be a way of attempting to move beyond or resolve past traumatic experiences.

> Trauma survivors may be drawn to similar situations and relationships because of the comfort inherent in familiarity.

In most cases, trauma is reenacted as a result of the psychological vulnerabilities and self-protective strategies characteristic of trauma survivors. The unfortunate bottom line is that trauma reenactment brings the past into the present in forms that continue to damage and disrupt one's life and relationships.

Considerations for Healing from Trauma, Treatment, and Recovery

Keep in mind that what happened to you in the past does not have the final say in who you become. For some people, trauma and its effect can heal on its own, after a period of time. For others, the healing process may require professional treatment. Recovery from trauma requires access to the conditions that promote healing. If an individual who has experienced trauma doesn't have access to recovery-supportive conditions, the effects of trauma may continue indefinitely and may even worsen.

Resolving trauma involves creating new neural pathways in the brain that reestablish the linkage between the limbic system and the neocortex. That makes it possible for a person to regain the ability to process traumatic events, make sense of them and the emotions with which they are connected, and place them in the appropriate context where they can be understood and integrated into his or her overall experience.

> Recovery from trauma requires access to the conditions that promote healing.

There are a variety of strategies, approaches, and actions that help to heal trauma and nurture the process of recovery. Some of these you can do on your own, while others involve professional treatment.

Trauma Self-Help Healing and Recovery Tips

Recovering from trauma takes time. It's so important to give yourself time to heal and to mourn the losses you've experienced related to your trauma. It's never helpful to try to force the healing process.

> Do the best you can to try to be patient with the pace of your healing and recovery.

Do the best you can to try to be patient with the pace of your healing and recovery. Be prepared to experience a variety of different trauma effects and symptoms described in this guidebook, including uncomfortable and intense emotions. Try to simply be aware of your thoughts and feelings, and allow yourself to feel whatever comes up without judgment, guilt or shame.

- **Minimize isolation by connecting with others.** Following a trauma, and especially when you are experiencing its effects, you may want to withdraw from others, but isolation makes things worse. Connecting with others can help you heal, so make an effort to maintain your relationships and avoid spending too much time alone.

- **Seek out support.** It's important to talk about your thoughts and feelings, and ask for help. Turn to a trusted family member, friend, counselor, or clergyman. Speak to family and friends. Support from family and friends can have a huge positive impact on coping with the trauma. It is often helpful to share thoughts and feelings with loved ones and friends. The twelve-step programs of recovery are among the most therapeutic sources of support available. If you are a member of a twelve-step program, it may be extremely helpful for you to increase your involvement by attending more meetings, speaking with your sponsor more frequently, and making greater use of your twelve-step support system. If you don't participate in a twelve-step program of recovery, now may be an excellent time to connect with one.

  It may be helpful to consider joining a support group for trauma survivors. Being with others who are facing the same problems can help reduce your sense of isolation and hearing how others cope can help inspire you. You may find you have a need to talk about the trauma over and over again. That's not uncommon, especially in the days and weeks after a traumatic event. That being said, if others try to talk with you about the trauma you've experienced but you find you are uncomfortable or simply prefer not to, then you have every right to gently refuse them.

- **Participate in social activities, even if you don't feel like it.** Try to continue with or resume your usual activities whether those are with others or by yourself. If you've retreated from activities or relationships that were once important to you, make the effort to reconnect with them. Schedule time for activities that bring you joy—favorite hobbies or activities with friends, for example.

Consider volunteering. As well as helping others, volunteering can be a great way to challenge the sense of helplessness that often accompanies trauma. Being of service by helping others in your family, your neighborhood or community, or a twelve-step program is a very effective way of taking the focus off yourself while serving as a reminder of your abilities and strengths. It can also help you reclaim a sense of competence and personal power.

> Trauma survivors are not to blame for the situation they find themselves in…

- **Minimize self-blame and judgment.** Trauma survivors are not to blame for the situation they find themselves in—you are not to blame for what happened to you. Instead of being angry with yourself, allowing yourself to be mired in guilt and/or shame, or blaming yourself for what happened to you or for your behavior during and after the traumatic event, try to be kind, compassionate, and forgiving toward yourself. Although reactions such as anger, guilt, anxiety, and depression are completely normal after trauma, blaming yourself will only make things more difficult. In the event you feel guilt, anger, or sadness, sharing these feelings with others may help you release them and give you access to the perspective of others.

- **Practice self-compassion.** Compassion means recognizing the pain of others and experiencing a desire to help to reduce their suffering—for example, offering understanding and kindness to others when they struggle, make mistakes, or fail. Expressing compassion is a spiritual experience that spreads outward whenever we can connect with another through shared experience. This can take many forms; including the awareness that pain, suffering, failure, and imperfection is universal to the experience of being human.

  Self-compassion consists of responding the same way toward yourself when you have a difficult time, experience pain, make mistakes, or experience something you don't like about yourself. Instead of harshly judging and criticizing yourself for your inadequacies, try to be kind and understanding with yourself. Having compassion for yourself means that you honor your humanness by accepting yourself when you struggle with challenges, including the effects of traumatic experiences. and fall short of your ideals or expectations.

- **Work on staying grounded in the here and now.** In order to maximize your ability to stay grounded, i.e., maintaining mental and emotional stability, after a trauma, it helps to have the consistency and predictability of a structured schedule to follow. As much as you can, maintain a daily routine (ideally the same schedule/routine you had prior to the trauma, assuming that still fits your needs), with regular times for waking up, sleeping, eating, working, and exercising. Make sure to schedule time for relaxing and social activities, too.

As much as you can, break large jobs into smaller, more manageable tasks. Focus on taking pleasure from the accomplishment of even small achievements. Find activities that make you feel better and keep your mind occupied (reading, taking a class, cooking, playing with your kids or pets), so you're not dedicating all your energy and attention to focusing on the traumatic experience.

Try to practice expressing gratitude. This may seem like a strange and off-putting idea in the aftermath of experiencing a traumatic event, but as described previously, gratitude promotes health and well-being. After a trauma, you may have to look harder to see the blessings in your life, but there are always things to be grateful for, no matter how negative or desperate the situation seems. You can learn, perhaps to your surprise, that it is possible to remain in conscious contact with gratitude in spite of the emotional pain and other uncomfortable effects of trauma.

• **Develop self-grounding skills through practice.** If the effects of your trauma include feeling fearful, anxious, full of rage, depressed, disoriented, or confused, it can be helpful to practice the following exercises.

> Sit in a chair with both feet on the ground and your hands on your thighs or in your lap. Feel your feet on the ground. Feel your hands on your thighs or lap. Feel your butt on the seat and your back against the chair.
>
> Look around you and pick out six objects in the room and name them out loud. This will help you to feel centered in the present, anchored in your body, and more grounded. When you do this, notice how your breathing begins to become smoother and deeper.
>
> You may want to go outdoors and find a peaceful place to sit. As you do, feel how your body can be held and supported by the ground. Notice the environment around you—the sky, the trees, the grass or other ground cover, and name them out loud.
>
> Wherever you are, take a look around. Don't look for anything particular or in a specific direction because you need to go someplace. Just look to see what is. Let your thoughts slow down as you name to yourself what you see. Start with the big picture. If you're inside: desk, walls, floor, ceiling, windows, chairs, tables, bookshelf, computer, bed, nightstand, etc. Then begin to take in smaller details: your own hands, your fingers, what they're touching. Take in the different shades of color and light. Use your other senses too. For instance, what do you hear? Do you hear the sounds of traffic, dogs barking, or birds outside?

> After a trauma, you may have to look harder to see the blessings in your life, but there are always things to be grateful for, no matter how negative or desperate the situation seems.

• **Take care of your health.** Because the mind and body are so closely connected, a healthy body also helps to improve your mental and emotional well-being and increases your ability to cope with the brain-based imbalances and other effects of trauma. Please refer to Pathways to Recovery, for more detailed information on healthy sleep hygiene, exercise, and nutrition.

✳ Get plenty of sleep. After a traumatic experience, anxiety and fear often disturb sleep patterns. A lack of sleep can contribute to a worsening of your trauma symptoms and make it harder to maintain emotional balance. Try to go to sleep and get up at the same time each day, and aim for seven to nine hours of sleep per night.

✳ The use of alcohol or other drugs may initially seem to help lessen your trauma symptoms, but as soon as the acute effects of alcohol and other drugs wear off, trauma symptoms usually get worse, with more intense feelings of depression, anxiety, and isolation.

✳ Exercise regularly. Regular exercise boosts serotonin, endorphins, and other natural feel-good brain chemicals. It also boosts self-esteem and helps to improve sleep. Whenever possible aim for thirty to sixty minutes of physical activity per day.

✳ Eat a well-balanced diet. Eating small, well-balanced meals throughout the day will help you keep your energy up and minimize emotional swings. While you may be drawn to sugary foods for the quick boost they provide, complex carbohydrates are a better choice. Foods rich in certain Omega-3 fats—such as salmon, walnuts, soybeans, and flaxseed—can help boost your mood.

• **Practice intentional breathing.** As explained in Pathways to Recovery, proper breathing is one of the master keys to good health. An important component of mindful self-awareness is an intentional focus on breathing that brings more oxygen into the bloodstream, which makes more oxygen available to internal organs and muscles. This can help reduce stress, lower blood pressure, improve digestion, increase blood circulation, decrease anxiety, and improve sleep and energy cycles. See Pathways to Recovery for more detailed information on intentional breathing.

Proper breathing is one of the master keys to good health.

- **Practice relaxation and stress reduction.** Relaxation and stress reduction exercises usually combine breathing and focused attention to calm the mind and the body. There are a wide variety of exercises you can practice and skills you can learn to activate your body's "relaxation response." Even practicing for a few minutes a day to start with can have noticeable benefits.

  Try approaches such as mindfulness, meditation, progressive muscle relaxation, yoga, or Chi Kung. Refer to Pathways to Recovery for more detailed information on mindfulness and meditation.

- **Become familiar with emotional regulation and distress tolerance and skills.** Allow yourself to feel what you feel when you feel it. Acknowledge your feelings about the trauma as they arise and accept them. The terms emotional regulation and distress tolerance skills come from Dialectical Behavior Therapy (DBT).

  Emotional regulation is related to mindfulness practice. It relates to identifying the emotions that are being felt in the moment and observing them without being overwhelmed by them. Emotional regulation skills include self-soothing activities that provide a calming effect and help to reduce emotional intensity such as the relaxation and stress-reduction practices mentioned above, as well as listening to music you enjoy, taking a walk, reading something pleasurable or spiritual, singing a favorite song, exercising, visualizing a comforting/relaxing image, journaling, etc. Emotional regulation is aimed at modulating feelings in order to strengthen the capacity to manage impulses so as to not behave in reactive, self-defeating, and destructive ways.

  Accepting your feelings is part of the grieving process and is necessary for healing from trauma. Learning how to be okay with uncomfortable emotions and allowing yourself to feel them is known as **distress tolerance.** Distress tolerance is about enduring and accepting discomfort, learning to bear pain skillfully. Distress tolerance skills are an outgrowth of mindfulness practices and involve the ability to nonjudgmentally accept both oneself and the current situation in spite of the emotional and physical distress experienced.

  It is important to clarify that acceptance does not equal approval. We can learn to tolerate thoughts, emotions, physical sensations, and situations we don't like at all and may even deeply dislike. Distress tolerance enhances coping capacity by strengthening resiliency—the ability to adjust to change.

- **Become an expert in trauma.** One of the most important tools in dealing with trauma is knowledge about the subject. The more you know about trauma, its consequences, and the ways to overcome it, the more likely you will be to handle what you are experiencing.

- **Coping with flashbacks.** As noted earlier, flashbacks are one of the effects of trauma. Flashbacks can be especially scary and upsetting because they seem so real. In the event you find yourself experiencing a flashback, you can be consciously aware of this. You can tell yourself you are having a flashback, and that it is okay and normal in people who have experienced trauma. Remind yourself that the worst is over; it happened in the past, but it is not happening now, even if you are reexperiencing some of it. "That was then, and this is now." However uncomfortable and upset you may feel, you survived *then*, which means you can get through what you are experiencing *now*.

  Ground yourself by becoming more aware of your environment in the present: stand up, stamp your feet, jump up and down, dance about, clap your hands. See where you are right now. Look around the room and notice the colors, the people, and the various objects. Make it more real. Notice and listen to the sounds around you: the traffic, voices, washing machine, music, etc. Notice the sensations in your body, the boundary of your skin, your clothes, the chair or floor underneath you. Pinch yourself or snap a rubber band on your wrist as a way of reinforcing the present and that the things you are reexperiencing occurred in the past.

  Take care of your breathing and breathe intentionally. Imagine you have a balloon in your stomach, inflating it as you breathe in, and deflating it as you breathe out. When we are anxious, scared, or stressed, our breathing automatically becomes more rapid and shallow. Sometimes this contributes to a sense of panic, as our body is not getting enough oxygen. This causes shakiness, light-headedness, and more panic. Breathing more slowly and deeply will help interrupt this process.

  Get support if you would like it. Let people close to you know about flashbacks so they can help if you want them to. That might mean holding you, talking to you, helping you to reconnect with the present, and to remember you are safe and cared for now.

  Flashbacks are powerful experiences, which drain your energy. Take time to look after yourself when you have had a flashback. You could have a warm, relaxing bath or a nap, a warm drink, play some soothing music, or just take some quiet time for yourself. When you feel ready, write down all you can remember about the flashback, and how you got through it. This will help you to remember information for your healing, and to remind you that you did get through it (and can again).

Professional Trauma Treatment

Healing from trauma frequently benefits from professional treatment. The ultimate purpose of treatment is to help free the individual from the grip of the effects of trauma and to help him or her begin to again live in the here and now, with an enhanced sense of safety, competence, and personal responsibility. Recovering from trauma that has progressed to PTSD generally requires professional assistance.

There are three fundamental phases to working through PTSD.

1. Stabilizing the person seeking treatment. Treatment in this phase focuses on helping him or her achieve a sense of safety, experience a reduction in distressing symptoms, and build awareness and skills.

2. Working through the traumatic experience. This involves going through the process of tolerating the discomfort of reviewing the traumatic events and memories.

3. Returning to daily life and routine. The therapist or other helping professional assists trauma survivors in applying their new understanding of themselves and their trauma experiences and using the skills they have developed to move forward in life.

Trauma treatment has experienced notable advances in recent years related to emerging work on the body-mind connection. For many years, trauma was treated almost exclusively with cognitively focused approaches, like Cognitive Behavioral Therapy (CBT). While CBT can be effective for people struggling with trauma, treatment is increasingly moving toward approaches that are more somatic because trauma is stored in the body.

Even when memories of the trauma are banished from the mind, trauma is always remembered in the body. Consequently, involving the body in the process of trauma healing is critical for most people. It is when the body feels safe that the brain is able to take in, process, and integrate new information and construct more current and complete realities that facilitate the healing process.

TRAUMA GROUNDING SKILLS AND REPROCESSING

Trauma grounding skills and reprocessing are skills used to help soothe anxiety by connecting you to the "here and now." They can help reduce defensive trauma responses, such as dissociation, flashbacks, and denial. Reducing such defensive responses helps trauma survivors experience a greater sense of safety and become more able to participate in process therapy for trauma issues. Grounding can be as simple as allowing trauma survivors to tell their story in a supportive and empathic environment that validates and normalizes one's trauma experiences and responses.

Systematic Desensitization

Systematic desensitization, sometimes called graduated exposure therapy, is a process that begins with learning coping strategies such as relaxation, breathing, visualization, and meditative skills. Once trauma survivors have these skills, they are placed in positions to put them to use when faced with stressors related to their traumatic experience(s). By successfully coping with progressively more intense exposure through practice, trauma survivors build awareness and skills that can make it possible to experience trauma-related stressors as less threatening and more manageable.

Somatic Experiencing

With somatic experiencing, the body uses its unique ability to heal itself. The emphasis of this form of therapy is on bodily sensations and learning to self-regulate rather than focusing on thoughts and memories about the traumatic event. By concentrating on what's happening in your body, trauma-related memory, energy, and tension may surface. Somatic therapy encourages releasing pent-up trauma-related energy through crying and other forms of physical release. Trauma survivors may gradually be able to deactivate the physical and emotional charge related to their traumatic experience(s).

Eye Movement Desensitization and Reprocessing (EMDR)

EMDR allows trauma survivors to reprocess memories and events. Reprocessing means that an individual accesses the relevant memory with the aid of bilateral stimulation of the right and left sides of the brain through eye movements, sounds, or tapping physically. This process helps to integrate trauma-related images, thoughts, emotion, and body sensations. EMDR can be used for other symptoms, such as anxiety or cravings. The rhythmic nature of this method is thought to assist with soothing the limbic system in the brain.

Cognitive Behavioral Therapy (CBT)

CBT can help trauma survivors process and evaluate thoughts and core beliefs about a trauma. While CBT doesn't treat the physiological effects of trauma, it can be extremely effective when used in addition to a somatically oriented therapy like somatic experiencing or EMDR.

CBT techniques are used to help individuals identify their maladaptive cognitive patterns and beliefs, such as discounting the positive in a situation by focusing on the negative; blowing things out of proportion; thinking in rigid black-and-white/all-or-nothing extremes; and placing unreasonable and unrealistic expectations on oneself, other people, and situations—"I should be better than this."

CBT seeks to replace such distorted thinking with more realistic and effective thoughts to reduce emotional distress and self-defeating behaviors. The process of replacing problematic cognitions with those that are more healthy and adaptive is referred to as cognitive restructuring. Cognitive restructuring is sometimes contrasted with **cognitive defusion**—a related but divergent set of techniques that draw on mindfulness practices and are emphasized in Acceptance and Commitment Therapy (ACT).

While the aim of cognitive restructuring via CBT is to actively change distressing thoughts and patterns of thinking, cognitive defusion focuses on observing and accepting uncomfortable thoughts without automatically buying into or attaching any particular value to them. Cognitive restructuring and cognitive defusion share a common foundation of bringing unhealthy automatic thinking to conscious awareness.

NOTES

ADDICTION AS A FAMILY DISEASE

Families today come in many varieties. There are families of origin, families by marriage, extended families, and families of choice. Some people are closer to a circle of friends than they are to those to whom they are connected by blood—those friends may effectively constitute a family. For the purposes of this section, we will use the words *family/families* to denote any and all of the persons in an addict's life who are close enough to the addict to be concerned with his or her recovery.

When you struggle with addiction and/or codependent caretaking, everything you experience and how you react to those experiences has the potential to either strengthen your recovery or pull you back toward active addiction/codependency. This section is designed to help you more clearly identify challenges and provide options, tools, and solutions that can help you make and maintain changes that improve the quality of your life.

Families as Systems

Families form systems that are much more than the individuals who comprise them. Every family has its own "organization," and family members develop particular ways of acting and reacting with each other and with the outside world. These patterns of interaction between family members give each family system a particular equilibrium and style related to such areas as expectations (spoken and unspoken); how feelings are expressed (or not); how conflict is managed (or avoided); how family issues are communicated in the world outside the family system; and what roles and responsibilities family members are assigned—consciously and unconsciously. These factors help shape the personality styles and behaviors of each family member.

Change in *any* part of the family system leads to changes in *all* parts of the system. Think of a mobile hanging from the ceiling in a child's room: when one part moves, all of the other parts move in response to it. As it relates to families, this process can work in a variety of ways. For example, when one family member—say, for instance, a parent—is overly responsible and controlling, this influences the attitudes and behaviors of other family members. They typically respond by becoming somewhat less responsible.

Conversely, when a family member struggles with active addiction, he or she usually under-functions and behaves irresponsibly. This too, shapes the behavior of other family members. They typically respond by becoming more controlling and overly responsible. The equilibrium or balance of the family system shifts as each member changes and adjusts accordingly. Whenever a family member struggles with a serious chronic condition, everyone in the family is significantly affected.

As a result, addiction affects the whole family. The havoc that active addiction creates in families and relationships negatively affects everyone in these "systems"—parents, children, siblings, spouses, partners, close friends, etc. The wreckage left in the wake of addiction has serious unhealthy consequences that impact everyone close to him or her.

> Whenever a family member struggles with a serious chronic condition, everyone in the family is significantly affected.

As a result, addiction really is a family disease. Active addiction frequently stresses the family system to the breaking point—destabilizing the home environment, disrupting family life, creating emotional pain, and wreaking havoc with mental and physical health, finances, and overall family dynamics. Without assistance and unless family members and significant others learn and practice how to do things differently, these effects can be chronic and long-term.

The addiction of a loved one brings up many difficult questions that may leave you unable to understand what is happening and why, and feeling like you are riding an emotional rollercoaster you can't get off. You may find yourself struggling with a number of painful and conflicting emotions, including guilt, shame, self-blame, frustration, anger, sadness, depression, anxiety, and fear.

No one, and no family, is immune from addiction. Like any other chronic disease, addiction to alcohol and other drugs afflicts people regardless of age, income level, educational background, race, ethnicity, religion/spirituality, sexuality, and community. *Anyone* can become addicted, and *anyone* can become affected by another person's addiction.

This material in this section is designed to provide information and options to those who, with or without conscience awareness, support the continued use of drugs (including alcohol) or other addictive behaviors by the addict in their lives. It will be of value to anyone who feels like they are trapped and to find freedom from the ongoing anguish of having a family member, partner, or close friend in active addiction.

What Exactly Is Addiction?

As described previously, addiction is one disease with many manifestations. Addiction can take many different forms and includes activities (such as gambling, sex, and eating), as well as alcohol and

> ### Addiction is a brain disease.

other drugs. All forms of the disease of addiction share certain universal characteristics, as well as progressive and predictable negative consequences.

People usually start using drugs or activities because it changes how they feel, and they like it. They don't plan to get addicted. At first, almost everyone believes they can control how much and how often they use. However, at a certain point the urge to use becomes too strong to control and people can't stop using even if they want to and know that using is causing harm to themselves and those who care about them. Using can become the most important priority in the person's life—everything else takes a back seat: school, work, previously important interests/hobbies, relationships that don't involve using, family, and even the need to eat or sleep. A person who is addicted might do almost anything to continue to be able to use.

Addiction is a brain disease. It is considered a disorder of the brain because addiction actually changes the brain's structure and functioning. The National Institute on Drug Abuse (NIDA) of the US Department of Health and Human Services defines addiction as a "chronic, relapsing brain disease characterized by compulsive drug seeking and use, despite harmful consequences."

> Brain imaging studies provide clear scientific evidence that addicts experience physical changes in the areas of their brains that involve judgment, decision-making, learning and memory, and behavior control. These changes affect how the brain works in extremely important ways. They help to explain the cycle of obsessive thinking, compulsive actions, and self-centered inability to delay gratification—including the decreased capacity to consider the consequences of one's actions—in which addiction traps those who struggle with it.

No one comes into this world knowing how to deal effectively with the addiction of a loved one. Fortunately, a process of recovery is also available to the family members and significant others of addicts to promote their own health and healing. This process involves becoming consciously aware of the specific ways in which addiction affects families and relationships and learning a new set of skills that must be practiced on an ongoing basis.

In Your Defense

The disease of addiction is both treacherous and seductive in the ways it attempts to convince those addicted that they don't have it. It is also resourceful in convincing family members and signficant others that their loved ones don't have it. After all, who wants to believe his or her spouse/partner, child, parent, sibling, or close friend is an addict?

As discussed in Roadblocks to Recovery, defense mechanisms are unconscious psychological processes that occur outside of our conscious awareness to help us cope with painful aspects of reality. Avoiding pain is healthy—up to a point. Defenses help make this happen through a process in the brain that results in paying less attention to, ignoring, or forgetting uncomfortable, disturbing thoughts, feelings, and situations. Everyone who struggles with addiction as well as their loved ones, are in significant discomfort and pain.

> Avoiding pain is healthy—up to a point.

For both addicts and their loved ones, *denial, minimizing, rationalizing, and avoidance* are the most commonly used defenses. People in active addiction rely on these defenses to protect themselves from the mental and emotional pain related to their using; family members rely on them to protect themselves from the mental and emotional pain related to their loved one's using. These defenses keep those struggling with addiction and their loved ones from being able to accurately see and admit many of the problems that are painfully obvious to others.

DENIAL

For their family members and significant others, denial takes the form of refusing to acknowledge their loved one has a problem because it would create too much anxiety, stress, or pain. Thinking or believing that addiction "won't happen to me" or "won't happen in my family/relationship" is another form of denial.

Describe an example of denial related to your loved one's addiction.

_____

_____

_____

_____

If you were watching yourself in denial on a video screen, what would you see?

_____

_____

_____

_____

MINIMIZING

Those with addicted loved ones often minimize the extent to which there is a problem. For example you might say, "John may drink and smoke pot, but he doesn't use 'hard drugs,'" "Tiffany just uses after school/work and on the weekends," or "He only takes pain meds prescribed by his doctor."

Describe an example of minimizing your loved one's using.

_____

_____

_____

_____

If you were watching yourself engaging in minimizing on a video screen, what would you see?

_____

_____

_____

_____

RATIONALIZING

Family members/significant others may admit their loved one has a problem, but it's "okay" and/or he or she is not responsible for it because:

1. He is just letting off steam after school or work.

2. She is in pain.

3. He is under a lot of stress.

4. She has been good lately or has been working really hard and so "deserves it."

If you were watching yourself attempting to rationalize on a video screen, what would you see?

_____

_____

_____

_____

AVOIDANCE

Avoidance, as previously discussed, is staying away from situations, people, or activities because they create anxiety, stress, or pain. It is about keeping distance from uncomfortable situations. Family members often avoid the obvious in an attempt to keep peace and avoid the discomfort of confrontation.

If you were watching yourself being avoidant on a video screen, what would you see?

_____

_____

_____

_____

Positive Intentions, Unintended Results

The desire to help others is an important human value. The desire to help those we love and to whom we are closest is natural and healthy. Parents want to help their children succeed; partners/spouses want to be helpful and supportive toward each other; and friends want to help each other deal with the various stresses and problems they encounter.

Unfortunately, often when family members, significant others, and friends attempt to help a loved one caught up in active addiction, the ways they go about it actually cause the problem to continue and get worse. This phenomenon is known as enabling.

Enabling

Enabling is the providing of assistance and support that perpetuates the problem rather than helps to solve it. It allows a person's active addiction to continue and progressively worsen. Enabling refers to anything a person does that helps the addicted individual avoid taking responsibility for his or her behavior, including the consequences of addiction.

Enabling frequently involves doing things or taking on responsibilities for someone else who could and should be taking care of him- or herself. Why would anyone enable a loved one in active addiction? There are a number of reasons.

1. The intention to help someone you love (as we noted earlier).

2. The desire to avoid facing the discomfort or pain of the problems that the addiction of someone you love has created.

3. The wish to exert some influence or control over a situation to "make it better."

> Enabling frequently involves doing things or taking on responsibilities for someone else who could and should be taking care of him- or herself.

In the short term, enabling behaviors seem to serve these purposes; however, over time, enabling becomes a lot like avoiding treating a cut on your leg (or the leg of a loved one) by scrubbing it with soap, water, and disinfectant because you know that taking these actions will hurt. The cut may seem like no big deal and nothing to be concerned about. But because its proper care is neglected, it slowly becomes infected. The infection spreads so gradually that its existence and progression may not be obvious; perhaps you don't even notice it.

Over time the infected cut becomes discolored, inflamed, and increasingly painful. You (or your loved one) begins to feel weak and feverish as the effects start to impair other aspects of health. At this point, the infection needs professional medical attention, probably treatment as an outpatient in a doctor's office.

If you or your loved one continue to deny and minimize the infection's significance and avoid seeking treatment, it will continue to get worse as the surrounding tissue begins to die. Now, much more intensive medical intervention is required. Without it, gangrene may set in, necessitating amputation and potentially placing you or your loved one's life at risk.

At that point, the infection must be effectively cut out through surgery, the area cleaned, and the patient treated with intravenous antibiotics. This process is costly, inconvenient, and painful. But without it, the infection will continue to progress, making recovery less possible, and premature death more likely.

Enabling behaviors come in many different forms (some of which may be very familiar to you), such as

- **Protecting:** From the natural consequences of his or her addiction

- **Secret Keeping:** Keeping the addict's behavior secret from others

- **Making Excuses:** Making excuses for the addict's behavior to yourself and others, such as family, friends, work, authorities, legal systems, school, etc.

- **Rescuing:** Getting the addict out of trouble by paying debts, bailing him or her out of jail, fixing tickets, paying his or her rent, calling his or her job, etc.

- **Blaming Others:** Blaming yourself or others, such as friends, girlfriends/boyfriends, job/boss, or family members for the addict's behavior

- **Rationalizing:** Seeing the "problem" and explaining it away as a result of something else, such as stress, job, depression, peers, family, health problems, etc.

- **Avoiding:** Either the addict or talking about issues related to his or her addiction in order to keep peace within the family or relationship

- **Giving Money:** Providing money that is unearned and undeserved and will likely fuel his or her addiction/using

- **Threats:** Making threats, but never actually following through on them

- **Doing for:** Doing things that he or she is fully capable of doing for him- or herself

Describe three instances when you have protected the addict in your life by helping him or her to avoid the natural negative consequences of his or her behavior.

1. _____

_____

_____

2. _____

_____

_____

3. _____

_____

_____

Describe an instance where you specifically kept the behavior of the addict in your life secret from others.

_____

_____

_____

Describe an instance where you made excuses for the addict's behavior to yourself and others.

_____

_____

_____

Describe an instance where you rescued the addict in your life by helping to get him or her out of financial or other trouble.

_____

_____

_____

Describe an instance where you blamed yourself or others for the addict's behavior.

_____

_____

_____

Describe two specific ways in which you have rationalized your loved one's addiction (where you saw there was a problem, but justified it to yourself and/or others as the result of something else, such as stress, job, depression, peers, family, health problems, etc.)

1. _____

_____

_____

2. _____

_____

_____

Describe two instances where you've avoided talking about issues related to your loved one's addiction in order to keep peace within the family or relationship.

1. _____

_____

_____

2. _____

_____

_____

Describe an instance when you provided money to the addict in your life to help him or her pay bills or debts that likely was used to fuel his or her addiction.

_____

_____

_____

As you know by now, those with addiction can be incredibly creative and manipulative in their efforts to fund their use of alcohol and other drugs, gambling, etc. Obviously, it's much easier for them to get money for bills, food, or shelter from family members/significant others/friends, rather than for drugs or whatever, even though chances are that's how any money they receive from you will be spent. Family members may secretly know this, but may give the money to the addict anyway, even though it perpetuates the addicted loved one's addiction.

As long as you give money to the addict in your life to pay bills, because he or she spent whatever money he or she had on drugs or addictive activities, keep in mind that no matter how much you lecture your addicted loved one and no matter how many promises he or she makes to change, it will continue to happen.

Describe two instances when you threatened your addicted loved one with some sort of consequence, but never actually followed through on it.

1. _____

_____

_____

2. _____

_____

_____

Describe two instances when you did things for the addict that he or she was fully capable of doing for him- or herself.

1. _____

_____

_____

2. _____

_____

_____

Attempting to "help" your addicted loved one in these ways may help you to feel more in control of what is essentially an out-of-control situation. However, this short-term benefit contributes to a longer-term cost, as these efforts to make the situation better allow it to continue to get worse.

> Enabling helps addicts dig themselves deeper into trouble.

Enabling helps addicts dig themselves deeper into trouble. Addiction is progressive. This means that over time active addiction increases in intensity, frequency, and severity as it consumes a greater percentage of time, attention, and energy. It always leads to problems in different areas of life, and those problems will become more and more serious.

The progression of addiction includes continuing to use alcohol and other drugs (and/or activities) despite increasingly serious negative consequences. These consequences include, but are not limited to, significant problems and losses related to family, relationships, health, employment, finances, and other interests.

By stepping in to try to fix your addicted loved one's problems, you decrease or even remove whatever motivation he or she may have to take responsibility for his or her own actions. Without that motivation, the addict in your life has little reason to consider changing, much less engage in the difficult and challenging work of recovery.

Codependency

Enabling behavior usually takes place in the larger context of a style of caretaking and relating to others known as codependency. Codependency is common in families with serious ongoing challenges—sometimes referred to as "dysfunctional families."

These families suffer from anxiety, fear, chronic stress, anger, pain, depression, guilt, shame, or trauma related to the existence of significant problems, such as:

- Addiction of a family member to alcohol and/or other drugs, gambling, food, sex/pornography, shopping/spending, Internet use, or work.

- Physical, sexual, or emotional abuse within the family.

- The presence of a family member with chronic physical or mental illness.

The major source of dysfunction in such families is that those problems and their effects on family members go unacknowledged and unaddressed. It's the proverbial "elephant in the living room." Everyone knows it's there and it takes up an incredible amount of space, yet some people act as if it doesn't exist.

Family members commonly describe feeling as if they are "walking on egg shells" and are "waiting for the other shoe to drop." This experience is both a cause *and* a result of ongoing stress and anxiety. In these families there are certain unspoken messages that are so prevalent they effectively become family rules.

- It's not okay or emotionally safe to talk about problems within the family, but even more so outside the family.

- Expressing emotions (other than perhaps anger) is a sign of weakness. Feelings should be kept to oneself.

- It's important to be "strong," "good," or "perfect."

- It's important to make the family look good, or at least "normal," to the outside world.

- "Don't rock the boat."

- And the ever popular, age-old favorite, "Do as I say, not as I do."

When people habitually enable/support this dysfunction they are considered codependent. You may be wondering, "Why would anyone do this? It makes no sense. It seems crazy!" The answer is that no one "wants" to do this.

Those with codependency are usually doing the best they can with the knowledge and experience they have. They're coping with extremely challenging and stressful circumstances as well as they can. Frequently, adults have learned these ways of coping through growing up in families with the same kinds of problems. They're trying to be helpful and protect themselves and other members of their family to the best of their current ability. This is especially relevant for women who, more often than not, assume the role of primary nurturers and caregivers in families and relationships—although it regularly applies to men as well.

Very rarely do people caught up in codependent caretaking think about it consciously. This process and the drive to participate in it happens unconsciously, underneath the surface of one's conscious awareness.

Codependency is defined as a pervasive and enduring pattern of focusing excessively on other people and their needs to the neglect of your own needs and interests. The term codependent is especially significant in that the person's sense of self, self-esteem, and sense of place in the world tends to be dependent on his or her relationships and willingness (and ability) to "help" everyone else. Codependency can afflict spouses/partners, parents, siblings, children, friends, or coworkers.

> Very rarely do people caught up in codependent caretaking think about it consciously.

In considering to what extent you may be codependent, please answer yes or no to the following questions:

_____ Do you often ignore unacceptable behavior?

_____ Do you find yourself taking on responsibilities that you later resent?

_____ Do you consistently put the needs and desires of others ahead of your own?

_____ Is it hard for you to identify and express your own emotions?

_____ Do you ever feel fearful that not doing something will cause a conflict or blow-up, lead to violence, or result in the other person leaving you?

_____ Do you ever lie to cover for someone else's mistakes?

_____ Do you assign blame for problems to other people rather than the one who is really responsible?

_____ Do you continue to offer help, even when it is taken for granted and unappreciated?

People who are codependent tend to have these characteristics:

1. Difficulty determining where their responsibility appropriately ends and the responsibility of others begins. As a result, they often have an exaggerated sense of responsibility for the actions of others.

2. A tendency to do more than their share much of the time.

3. A tendency to become hurt when people don't recognize their efforts, including efforts no one has requested.

4. An unhealthy dependence on relationships. One form this takes is going to extraordinary lengths to hold on to a relationship.

5. Fear of abandonment and of being alone.

6. A tendency to sacrifice their own needs to accommodate other people.

7. A tendency to communicate indirectly due to discomfort when directly expressing his or her own needs and desires.

8. A sense of guilt when asserting themselves and their own needs.

9. A consistent need to control others. This often takes the form of manipulating, cajoling, promising, pleading, and bargaining.

10. Difficulty trusting themselves and others.

11. Difficulty identifying and expressing feelings.

12. Difficulty being honest with their feelings due to a strong need for approval.

13. People pleasing, e.g., setting limits and saying "no" to others causes anxiety and stress.

14. Underlying anger that usually comes out passive aggressively.

15. Difficulty making decisions.

Describe how each of these characteristics applies to you.

1. _____

_____

_____

2. _____

_____

_____

3. _____

_____

_____

4. _____

_____

_____

5. _____

_____

_____

6. _____

_____

_____

7. _____

_____

_____

8. _____

_____

_____

9. _____

_____

_____

10. _____

_____

_____

11. _____

_____

_____

12. _____

_____

_____

13. _____

_____

_____

14. _____

_____

_____

15. _____

_____

_____

Codependency interferes with the ability to have healthy, reciprocal, mutually satisfying relationships. It can be a contributing factor in chronic dissatisfaction, anxiety, depression, and physical illness.

THE SIMILARITIES BETWEEN CODEPENDENCY AND ADDICTION

Like addiction, codependency affects people mentally, emotionally, behaviorally, and spiritually. Because of the obsessive thoughts and compulsive behaviors that characterize codependent caretaking, codependency can be considered a manifestation of addiction. In fact, codependency is sometimes thought of as a form of **relationship addiction** because it keeps people stuck in relationships that are one-sided and often abusive.

In codependency, attention is obsessively and compulsively focused on other people and their needs. Obsession is thinking about something over and over and over, even when you don't want to, like a song stuck on repeat that won't stop playing. A compulsion is an overpowering impulse to do something, to act obsessively.

People with codependency spend an extraordinary amount of time thinking about other people or relationships. They can also become obsessed when they think they've made or might make a "mistake." The need to do for others, to try to help and protect them (even when that assistance is unappreciated and unwanted) is a form of compulsion.

SELF-ESTEEM STRUGGLES

People who are codependent usually struggle with low self-esteem and feelings of self-worth. Often they feel not good enough, somehow less than others, or simply not enough. However, it's helpful to be aware there is also another side to low self-esteem—often people seem arrogant and think highly of themselves when this is really a way to cover up and compensate for feeling inadequate or unlovable. Hidden from conscious awareness are feelings of guilt and shame, along with a need for perfectionism.

When the goal of solving the problems or relieving the pain of others is met, the codependent person's self-esteem rises. Positive feelings come from being liked and accepted by others. They need other people to like them to feel okay about themselves. In this sense, other people are the codependent person's "drug." While the circumstances certainly are different, this is essentially the same dynamic experienced by those in active addiction.

After using for some time, addicts must get their "fix," not so much to get high, but just so they can feel okay. Codependents need to get their "fix" through focusing on others in order to feel okay. The identity and self-worth of codependents is so dependent on other people, that not being involved in the lives of others makes them feel emotionally rejected and abandoned.

> When the goal of solving the problems or relieving the pain of others
> is met, the codependent person's self-esteem rises.

Codependent individuals have a need to control those close to them because they need other people to behave in certain ways to feel okay. Control helps people with codependency feel emotionally safe and secure. Obsessively trying to please other people (also known as people pleasing) and compulsively taking care of them can be used to control and manipulate.

BOUNDARY BLURRING

Boundaries are sort of an imaginary line between you and others that separates what belongs to you from what doesn't, and applies not only to your possessions, money, and body, but also to your thoughts, feelings, and needs. Codependency blurs these boundaries when people take responsibility for the problems and feelings of others and/or attribute responsibility for their own problems and feelings to others.

Another effect of blurred or porous boundaries is that people who are codependent take responsibility for meeting the perceived needs of others at the expense of their own needs. If someone else has a problem, individuals with codependency not only put that person ahead of themselves, but they must help to the point where they feel rejected if their help is unwanted. Because this need is so great, they often keep trying to help and fix the other person.

People with codependency are often highly reactive. In other words, they react rapidly to the expressed thoughts and feelings of others. People with codependency tend to personalize what happens around them, seeing most everything as being directly related to them. If you are codependent and someone says something you disagree with, you immediately either believe it completely or become upset and defensive. You tend to absorb the words of others, rather than recognize that what they said is merely their opinion and may not have anything to do with you.

> Boundaries are sort of an imaginary line between you and others...

People who are codependent tend to have unrealistic expectations of themselves and have difficulty accepting their own realistic limitations. As a result, they often view themselves as failures when they cannot control situations to their satisfaction or meet everyone's expectations.

Codependency creates problems with intimacy. This is connected to anxiety and fear about being judged, rejected, or abandoned. In this context, intimacy is not about sex so much as it refers to the capacity to have an open, honest, and emotionally close and connected relationship with another person.

Turning the Corner

Over time, the world of the codependent usually becomes smaller and smaller as their social circles diminish and their focus on addicted loved ones increases and becomes more obsessive, while the need to take care of or try to control their loved one becomes more compulsive. If any of this sounds or feels familiar to you, it simply means that you are in the right place.

If you believe your addicted loved one is *the* problem, and you believe he or she needs to change in order for you to feel better, then you have given up responsibility for your own feelings. By turning over responsibility for your feelings to someone else, you are basically giving them control over how you feel in any given moment. Consider the ramifications of this when you put how you feel in the hands of an addicted person.

Whether you experience peace of mind, happiness, a sense of well-being, or whatever, is dependent on someone else—in this instance, the person with addiction. It will be difficult for you to be okay within yourself as long as you are focused on what you cannot change, namely other people and situations.

You try to change the other person because his or her behavior is unhealthy and often hurtful, and you may fear others will view his or her embarrassing behavior as a negative reflection on you. Trying to change the addict in your life can also help provide you with the illusion of having more control over the situation than you actually do.

> It will be difficult for you to be okay within yourself as long as you are focused on what you cannot change…

You try to figure out why the other person acts the way he or she does. You are genuinely confused as to why your loved one keeps saying he or she will change, but never does. You may feel hurt because your loved one doesn't keep his or her promises and won't change for you (after all, look at all you have done and continue to do for him or her). In order for the situation to get better there is another illusion you will need to let go of. This illusion is the belief that "I would be just fine, if *only* _____ would just change. I only think, feel, and act this way because of _____." If you place your own sense of self-worth in the hands of an actively addicted person it's no wonder why life seems so frustrating, chaotic, and crazy.

Codependency is built on a foundation of coping mechanisms that are ultimately self-defeating. Ironically, the intent of these coping mechanisms is two-fold—to help you better manage situations with your addicted loved one and to minimize you own emotional pain. As a result, these coping mechanisms—which may work at first, but sooner or later only make things worse—become a habit that evolves into a survival strategy. This survival strategy is frequently transmitted from one generation to the next, in which unconsciously children learn it from observing and interacting with their parents.

For most people, change is difficult and scary. There is a natural fear of the unknown and the uncertainty that goes hand-in-hand with it. It can be hard to do anything that's different or unfamiliar because anything that is unfamiliar tends to be uncomfortable. And the more different or unfamiliar it is, the more uncomfortable it tends to be. It takes strength and courage to do anything that is uncomfortable. That's why doing things differently from the way you've done them in the past always takes strength and courage.

Family Recovery

You many be thinking, *Why do I need to change anything? He's the problem!* Among the greatest challenges family members and significant others face in getting help for themselves is that they continue to believe everything will be okay if only they can fix their addicted loved one. And as long as they stick to this belief, the problem continues to get worse.

For the family members of addicted individuals, the basic foundation of recovery is the awareness and acceptance that as part of the family system that has allowed the problem (active addiction) to continue, you have been effectively part of "the problem." This realization may be difficult and painful for you. You may still want to throw this book down and scream, "But I'm not the problem, my son/daughter/husband/wife/partner/friend/coworker, etc. is the one who needs help, not me!" I am not suggesting that *you* are the problem. What you will need to accept is that the only part of the problem that you have the ability to change is *your* part.

Obviously, you certainly didn't cause your loved one's problem and your experience to this point has clearly shown you can't control the problem; however, there are ways in which you have unknowingly contributed to the problem.

The reality is that the only thing you can change is you, and this is the essence of the recovery process—whether for someone in active addiction or their family members and significant others.

Since addiction affects the family members of those addicted, long-term recovery for these addicted individuals is most successful when their family members participate in a process of recovery for themselves. Just as your addicted loved one is responsible for his or her recovery, you are responsible for your recovery. The most important thing you can do to help your addicted family member or significant other is to make a commitment to getting help and support for yourself.

What Is Recovery for Family Members/Significant Others?

Recovery (regardless of what people are recovering from) is a process of change. This process of change includes learning how to think and act differently. After all, *the only way to get different results is to do things differently.*

Recovery involves learning, growth, and healing. Recovery is the process by which a person learns and practices new patterns of living—developing the awareness and building the skills to live a whole, healthy, and healed life. Being in recovery means that a person is participating in life activities that are healthy, meaningful, and fulfilling for them.

> Recovery involves learning, growth, and healing.

It will help you to better understand if you look at this process as an ongoing journey of becoming consciously aware of self-defeating thoughts and behaviors and replacing them with growth-enhancing ways of relating to yourself, others, and the world.

This might sound overwhelming; recovery is difficult and can be extremely challenging. Like all large and intimidating projects, it works best when the process is broken down into smaller, more manageable pieces. How do you eat an elephant? One *bite* at a time. In a similar fashion, recovery is a life-long process, which takes place one *day* at a time.

Similar to working out physically, progress requires learning how to go through a certain degree of discomfort and pain. Like other areas of life, the greatest growth comes from pushing yourself to go beyond the boundaries of familiarity and comfort you have constructed over the years. Recovery is about taking care of *you* in a healthy manner and moving gradually and progressively toward balance emotionally, physically, mentally, and spiritually. This journey of recovery can help you learn how to be okay within yourself no matter what is going on outside of you.

While there are many things you can do in support of recovery—both for yourself and your addicted loved one—he or she will have to make the final decision as to whether and when to seek a healthier and better life or to continue on the self-destructive path of active addiction. At this point you understand you can't control his or her behavior. However, there are certain approaches you can take that can influence his or her actions and increase his or her chances of recovery. In the process, you can pursue your own recovery process and learn how to take better care of yourself and your own needs.

ALLOW NATURAL CONSEQUENCES TO OCCUR

It is important to let your addicted loved one experience the natural consequences of his or her actions. "Natural" consequences refer to the problems and other negative results of a person's involvement in active addiction. Allowing your addicted loved one to experience the naturally occurring consequences of his or her addiction-related behavior may seem like some sort of punishment, but it isn't. It need not come from a place of cold and/or angry distancing.

Quite the contrary, it can come from a place of caring, compassion, and love based on the awareness that your addicted loved one can benefit from experiencing those consequences and what they teach him or her. His or her actions and their consequences belong to him or her, not to you. Those teaching moments can increase his or her motivation to make positive and healthy changes. When you allow your loved one to experience the consequences of his or her actions you give him or her the opportunity to learn a powerful lesson that he or she may not be able to learn any other way.

Describe what you can do to begin to let your addicted loved one experience the natural consequences of his or her addiction (be specific):

_____

_____

_____

_____

DETACH WITH LOVE

Allowing your addicted loved one to experience the naturally occurring consequences of his or her active addiction is part of loving detachment. When family members and significant others learn about the need for "detachment," they often find it confusing, anxiety provoking, and extremely uncomfortable. Many interpret detachment as being unsupportive and rejecting of their addicted loved one. At first some even see it as abandonment. In reality, however, when you detach from your addicted loved one with love and compassion, you begin to create healthy emotional, as well as practical, boundaries for yourself.

Detachment isn't "all or nothing." It does not mean having nothing to do with your addicted loved one. You do not have to totally detach from him or her, only from certain areas of his or her life.

> …when you detach from your addicted loved one with love and compassion, you begin to create healthy emotional, as well as practical, boundaries for yourself.

Detachment in this sense is separating the addicted person from his or her addictive behaviors, and intentionally responding to the person rather than to their behaviors. Detachment with love means caring enough about other people to allow them to learn from their mistakes. It also acknowledges your own lack of control over the other person's addictive behaviors and communicates that your addicted loved one is responsible for his or her own choices and actions.

To detach with love is to develop the ability to care deeply about your addicted loved one from a kind and compassionate, but objective, position. It means caring while not being so emotionally invested in or controlled by your addicted loved one's actions and how he or she reacts to you and the decisions you need to make.

Letting others take care of their own affairs, not doing for them what they need to do for themselves, is detachment. Not immersing yourself in trying to prevent a crisis caused by your addicted loved one's behavior is detachment. Letting go of the need to manipulate or control others to carry out some aspect of their lives according to your wishes is detachment.

> **Describe what you can do to begin to detach from your addicted loved one with love (be specific).**

_____

_____

_____

_____

Detaching with love is healthy for you and your family as a whole, as well as for your addicted loved one. You and your family have effectively been held mental and emotional hostage by your addicted love one. Detachment helps free you from this form of captivity.

Because detachment is such a different experience for family members and significant others of addicted loved ones, it at first feels confusing, weird, and extremely uncomfortable—maybe even painful. It may be difficult for you to not think about your addicted loved one obsessively or you may experience even stronger feelings of anxiety and emptiness.

As challenging as detaching with love can be, when you allow yourself to go through the discomfort of this process and not get pulled back into familiar (and in turn, comfortable) patterns of enabling and codependent caretaking, the enhanced sense of freedom and self-esteem you experience will surprise you.

> **If you were to watch yourself on a video screen after successfully detaching with love from your addicted loved one, what would you see (be specific)?**

_____

_____

_____

_____

_____

GIVE THE GIFT OF YOUR ATTENTION TO OTHER FAMILY MEMBERS

As you know all too well, focusing on the addiction of a loved one can consume an incredible amount of your time and energy. It is easy to become lost in the whirlwind of crisis, intensity, and negativity of active addiction and unintentionally make other family members a lower priority. You don't mean for it to happen, but these other family members—whether they are your (other) children or your spouse/partner—are often neglected by default. They understandably feel ignored or less important because so much attention is focused on the addict.

Anxiety, stress, and drama take their toll on the marriage/primary relationship and the family as a whole. In addition to making time for yourself and space for your needs, make a conscious effort to use some of the time and energy freed up by detaching with love from your addicted loved one to spend quality time with your other loved ones.

The Therapeutic Value of Connection and Support through Mutual Aid/ Twelve-Step Programs

Active addiction and codependency are isolating conditions that tend to disconnect those afflicted from other people. Over time, as these conditions progress, most people gradually separate from relationships that were previously important—with family, friends, coworkers, and other sources of social connection and potential support. The guilt and shame that go hand-in-hand with both active addiction and having an addicted family member/partner is a contributing factor in this process. Many people who struggle with an addicted loved one feel unique and very much alone in their experience. Most think, *No one knows what I've been through and what I've had to do, and certainly no one could possibly understand my situation.*

Although some people with codependency seem needy, others act like they're completely self-sufficient and have no interest in or need for assistance. They may help everyone else but they have no need for help themselves. These individuals have great difficulty reaching out and being on the receiving end of help. Moreover, in the United States we place great importance on being self-reliant or self-sufficient. As a result, needing help, even in extraordinary, crisis-oriented circumstances, is sometimes viewed as "weakness." And who wants to seem weak?

Yet, similar to those in recovery from addiction to alcohol and other drugs, recovering from codependency requires a great deal of support and help. Recovery necessitates finding the strength to realize that no matter how capable and self-sufficient you may be, you need help mobilizing the courage to reach out and actually seek the help you need. The most effective vehicles for recovery-related support and assistance are mutual-aid programs, particularly twelve-step programs or professional help in the form of counseling or a combination of both.

Humans are social beings. We are hardwired for relationships, to be connected with other people. A fundamental aspect of making time for yourself and space for your own needs, as part of your recovery, is connecting with others who have been through similar experiences and are at various stages on the road to recovery. Developing a network of support is crucial to the recovery process.

Mutual-aid programs are nonprofessional organizations where members meet in groups and share about their experiences and voluntarily support one another. Mutual-aid groups provide participants social, emotional, and informational support aimed at understanding and taking responsibility for their attitudes and actions and grow toward health and healing.

TWELVE-STEP PROGRAM PARTICIPATION

Twelve-step programs are the most successful and widely available resource for individuals seeking recovery. Twelve-step programs use a mutual-support approach to recovery from addictive and other obsessive-compulsive conditions, based on a set of guiding principles. Research demonstrates that practicing the Twelve Steps has a profound and positive impact on life functioning. Twelve-step programs for the family members, partners, children, and friends of those struggling with addiction such as Al-Anon, Nar-Anon, and Co-Dependents Anonymous (CODA), came about in response to increased understanding that addiction affects everyone close to it, and is often enabled by well-meaning significant others.

Adult Children of Alcoholics (ACA) is a twelve-step program encompassing a diverse group of recovering people that includes adult children of alcoholics/addicts, people struggling with codependency, and those challenged with a variety of different forms of addiction. In ACA, the term "adult child" is used to describe adults who grew up in families with addiction or significant dysfunction such as domestic violence, abuse, abandonment, neglect, etc. ACA is among the few twelve-step programs that directly address trauma within one's family of origin.

It's helpful to be aware that in some ways, recovery from codependent caretaking is even more complicated than recovery from addiction related to addictive substances or behaviors. Whether an addicted person is using is clear¾he or she either is or is not. If he or she relapses it is objective and measurable. In contrast, for those in recovery from codependency, defining where legitimate concern ends and obsessive worrying begins is much more difficult. It is a difference in degree along a continuum that ranges from healthy to problematic. Moreover, it's possible to experience a relapse of worry, anger, resentment, self-pity, guilt, or shame or other negative emotions before you realize what has happened. Access to the knowledge and experience of others who have first-hand experience with all phases of codependency and recovery is an invaluable resource.

Al-Anon, Nar-Anon, CODA, and ACA are based on behavioral, cognitive, and spiritual principles and practices that help people progress toward recovery and maintain it one day at a time. These principles and practices are contained in the Twelve Steps and include:

1. Admitting powerlessness over the addicted loved one and that your efforts to help him or her made your life unmanageable.

2. Acknowledging that willpower alone cannot achieve and sustained recovery and that help is necessary.

3. Connecting to others who have been through similar experiences is essential to combat isolation and provide social support and mutual aid.

4. Having faith in a power beyond oneself (left to one's own definition).

5. Letting go of the need to try to control people and situations.

6. Examining past errors with the help of a sponsor (an experienced member who serves as a mentor).

7. Making amends for those errors.

8. Recovery includes a process of spiritual renewal that uses the tools of meditation, prayer, and applying spiritual principles; and being of service by helping others who want to achieve recovery.

As effective as the twelve-step programs of recovery have proven to be—more people have achieved and maintained recovery from addiction through twelve-step programs than any other method, by far—they aren't perfect. They have their critics, and you may encounter unhelpful individuals or aspects of twelve-step recovery that rub you the wrong way. If you look for reasons to complain or not participate, you will find them, the same as in any other area of life.

It is not uncommon for people to find attending twelve-step meetings uncomfortable, at least at first. You are encouraged to attend different meetings in order to find those that best fit you. New experiences are often uncomfortable and adjusting to them usually takes some time.

Even though spirituality is an important area of life, for some, the focus on spirituality in twelve-step programs can be a turn-off. It's important to keep in mind that twelve-step programs are spiritual, not religious. For some twelve-step program members, spirituality and religion are connected, but for many they are not. There are atheists who have been in recovery for decades in twelve-step programs. The twelve-step process of recovery allows you the freedom to choose what form your spirituality will take, based on the right fit for you.

For people seeking recovery, twelve-step programs provide a widely available and remarkably effective support system by surrounding them with people who have gone through, and are going through, the same struggles. The hope, support, and encouragement that can only be provided by those who have grown beyond enabling behaviors and codependent caretaking to build successful long-term recovery for themselves, is of unparalleled therapeutic value.

Twelve-step programs provide the opportunity to develop new and healthier relationships, build new friendships based on significant shared values and goals, and help you learn or relearn how to have fun.

When was the last time you remember having fun?

Twelve-step programs create an environment that promotes emotional safety, where people experience being connected and feeling understood and accepted.

There are many individual differences among the people at any given twelve-step meeting, however, addiction and codependent caretaking are powerful equalizers, and a shared interest in recovery brings together a wide variety of people who may look different on the outside but share many of the same experiences and challenges.

The commonalities among people who struggle with codependent caretaking and the goal of learning how to live differently—free from unhelpful and unhealthy patterns—can generate a connection that translates to deep mutual understanding, acceptance, and support in recovery.

HELP YOUR CHILDREN GET THE HELP THEY NEED

In families where addiction or other dysfunction is present and problems are typically either denied or covered up, children need special attention, guidance, and support. Children in such families have high levels of confusion and stress, and need to have their experiences validated. They need to be able to feel emotionally and physically safe.

> Children need reliable adults whom they can trust and in whom they can confide…

It is important to talk openly and honestly with your children about what is happening in your family and to create an environment where they can feel safe to express their concerns and feelings. It can be valuable to consult with professional counselors/therapists more specifically about what and how much to share with your children based on their age(s) and ability to understand. Children need reliable adults whom they can trust and in whom they can confide—adults who will support them, reassure them, and provide them with help appropriate to their age and developmental stage.

Children living with addiction can benefit from a range of helpful resources. Besides counseling at school or in the community, there may be educational support groups available in their school. Children who are age eleven and older can join Alateen groups, which meet in community settings and provide healthy connections with others coping with similar issues. Alateen is twelve-step fellowship of young Al-Anon members, usually teenagers, whose lives have been affected by someone else's addiction.

Self-Care and Balance

If you want to recover, taking care of yourself must be a high priority. When you travel by air, and prior to take off, the flight attendants go over the various emergency procedures. They announce that in the event of a loss of cabin pressure and the overhead oxygen masks deploy, should you be traveling with someone who needs assistance with his or her mask (for example, a child) *always* put your oxygen mask on first. Do so before you attempt to help someone else. What is the reason for this specific instruction? If you don't take care of your own mask first and you encounter complications/problems while helping another person, you are at greater risk of passing out and getting injured or potentially dying from lack of oxygen.

This same concept applies to your taking care of yourself in recovery. If you don't take good enough care of yourself, you won't be of much use or help to anyone else and you may put yourself at risk.

Self-care means paying conscious attention to, and taking care of, your own immediate needs. This includes returning to people, interests, and activities that were once important in your life—things that helped give your day-to-day experience enjoyment, meaning, and value—before you lost yourself in the series of crises that come with having an addicted loved one and becoming stuck in the web of codependent caretaking.

> Self-care means paying conscious attention to, and taking care of, your own immediate needs.

Because addiction and codependency affect people mentally, emotionally, physically, and spiritually, recovery needs to include mental, emotional, physical, and spiritual elements. Refer to the Four Points of Balance previously discussed in Pathways to Recovery, for a more in-depth discussion.

NOTICING AND OBSERVING YOUR THOUGHTS

Recovery includes becoming consciously aware of your thought process to allow for acknowledgement and recognition of your thoughts without reacting to them automatically or impulsively. With practice, you will be able to witness your thoughts as they arise in your awareness. This level of awareness gives you an opportunity to make a conscious decision as to how much or how little credibility to give your thoughts at any moment in time.

 Take a few moments and observe your thoughts as they come up for you right now. Write down two that come to mind (whatever those thoughts may be).

1. _____

_____

_____

2. _____

_____

_____

Describe to what extent these thoughts are accurate and relevant to your needs right now; or are they merely stories that distract you and take your attention away from something more immediate and important?

1. _____

_____

_____

2. _____

_____

_____

We can't avoid pain, but we do have a choice how we respond to our painful emotions.

Take a little time each day to practice consciously observing your thoughts and consciously considering to what extent they are accurate and helpful versus distracting and unhelpful. Make a little time each day to practice identifying and letting yourself feel your feelings. When we are caught up in our feelings—especially powerful distressing ones such as anxiety, fear, sadness, depression, guilt, shame, frustration, anger, loneliness, and grief—they sometimes seem as though they will last *forever*. However, whether they are positive or painful, feelings are always *temporary*. We can't avoid pain, but we do have a choice how we respond to our painful emotions.

Describe one thing you can do to exercise greater conscious choice in how you respond to uncomfortable or painful feelings.

_____

_____

_____

_____

Take a little time each day to practice consciously observing your emotions. Simply becoming consciously aware of your emotions—realizing that you are experiencing feelings and identifying what the feelings are, allows you enough separation from them to give you the opportunity to choose how best to take care to them. Developing emotional balance will help you gradually let go of whatever guilt and shame you have carried with you like heavy luggage related to your loved one's addiction.

Diet and exercise are an essential element of a strong recovery program and promotes balance in all areas of life. Take a moment to review the material in Pathways to Recovery, before answering the following questions.

Describe your current daily dietary and nutritional routine—what and how frequently you eat on average.

_____

_____

_____

_____

What changes in terms of eating a balanced mix of foods can you begin now to improve the quality of your diet and nutrition?

_____

_____

_____

_____

What changes in terms of adjusting portions (the amount of different foods you eat) can you begin now to improve the quality of your diet and nutrition?

_____

_____

_____

_____

SLEEP

Sleep is as important to health, well-being, and recovery as air, food, and water. Take some time to describe your pre-sleep routines.

What do you do prior to going to sleep? If you were watching yourself on a video screen during the last thirty to sixty minutes before you go to bed, what would you see (be specific)?

_____

_____

_____

_____

_____

Describe how your pre-sleep routines are likely to promote or obstruct sleep.

_____

_____

_____

_____

Describe two changes you can begin to make now to improve your sleep hygiene and give yourself opportunities to sleep better.

1. _____

_____

_____

2. _____

_____

_____

INTENTIONAL BREATHING

Proper breathing is one of the master keys to good health. It is also a connection to all of the Four Points of Balance. An important component of mindful self-awareness, intentional, conscious focus on breathing can achieve remarkable results: reducing stress, lowering blood pressure, improving digestion, increasing blood circulation, decreasing anxiety, and improving sleep and energy cycles.

How is it that intentional breathing—sometimes referred to as breathwork—can have such a powerful effect on our health? Unlike any other function of the body, breathing is the only one we do both voluntarily and involuntarily. As such, it is the only function through which we can access and influence the autonomic (involuntary) nervous system, which regulates the heart, circulation, digestion, and other vital functions. Imbalances in the autonomic nervous system are the root cause of many ailments, including hypertension, chronic stress, and disorders of circulation and digestion, to name a few.

> Proper breathing is one of the master keys to good health.

BREATHING BASICS

1. Observe and follow your breath. Focus your attention on your breathing, without trying to influence it.

2. Make your breathing deeper, slower, and quieter. Taking slow, deep breaths is a quick and easy stress-reduction technique.

3. Breathe abdominally. When you inhale and take a breath in, focus on expanding your belly rather than your chest. Breathing through your stomach will help your breathing become deeper, slower, and quieter.

4. Exhale/squeeze out more air. It is important to keep in mind that you deepen your breathing primarily by exhaling more air, not inhaling more. If you can push more air out of your lungs, your lungs will automatically take more in.

✎ Describe a change you can begin to make *now* to become more aware of your breathing.

_____

_____

_____

Describe a change you can begin to make *now* to use your breathing to improve your levels of physical and overall balance.

_____

_____

_____

RELAXATION

Relaxation exercises generally combine breathing and focused attention to calm the mind and the body. There are a wide variety of relaxation exercises that you can learn to activate your body's "relaxation response." The relaxation response is the opposite of the "fight-or-flight" reaction that prepares your body for rapid action in response to perceived threats. The relaxation response helps to reduce and even reverse the physical, mental, and emotional effects of stress. Activating the relaxation response helps to facilitate the experience of that all-important but often illusive quality of serenity/inner peace/peace of mind.

Ongoing stress makes us more susceptible to illness and disease. It saps energy and contributes to fatigue, negative thinking, and distressing emotions, including anxiety, fear, frustration, anger, self-pity, and depression. According to medical research, stress is responsible for as much as 90 percent of all illnesses and diseases—most notably hypertension, heart disease, and cancer. In addition, stress can be a contributing factor in making existing medical conditions worse. Ongoing/chronic stress interferes with your attitude, social and family relationships, work, health, and of course, recovery. As a result, learning and practicing ways to facilitate relaxation in order to counteract the stress you experience is vital to health, balance, and recovery.

Ongoing stress makes us more susceptible to illness and disease.

There are a variety of techniques and self-soothing activities that can facilitate relaxation, provide a calming effect, and help to reduce emotional intensity, including but certainly not limited to: listening to music you enjoy, taking a walk, reading something pleasurable or spiritual, singing a favorite song, exercising, visualizing a comforting/relaxing image, journaling, and meditation. Refer to Pathways To Recovery and Trauma, Addiction, and Recovery for detailed discussions of a range of relaxation and self-calming practices.

What, if any, activities to you participate in currently that help you to feel more relaxed and reduce your level of stress?

_____

_____

_____

_____

What, if any, activities in the past helped you feel more relaxed and reduced your level of stress that you no longer participate in?

_____

_____

_____

_____

Identify three changes you can begin to make *now* to help you feel more relaxed and reduce your level of stress.

1. _____

_____

_____

2. _____

_____

_____

3. _____

_____

_____

> Spiritual balance helps people find meaning and purpose, even in situations that are uncomfortable and painful.

SPIRITUAL BALANCE

Spirituality is concerned with matters of the spirit, those aspects of life beyond oneself. It includes a sense of connection with others, and to the world around you—an experience of being part of a greater whole. Spirituality emphasizes the commonalities that all people share that link us together. It provides an antidote for the experience of feeling different and disconnected from others, and from the world. Spiritual balance helps people find meaning and purpose, even in situations that are uncomfortable and painful.

What does spirituality means to you?

_____

_____

_____

_____

_____

Describe your current practice of spirituality.

_____

_____

_____

_____

_____

There are many practices that can contribute to and enhance spiritual balance. These include but are certainly not limited to prayer and meditation.

PRAYER

Spiritual traditions from around the world incorporate forms of prayer. Many people maintain a belief in the healing power of prayer. Prayer can take many different forms. Sometimes it is formal and other times it is informal. Your process of prayer may take a specific form or consist of simple communication in a conversational manner with your higher power. Regardless of whether you practice of prayer comes from an established religion, or elsewhere, or you have come up with your own form(s) of it, the act of communication with that beyond oneself is the intention.

MEDITATION

Meditation quiets the mind by helping to still the ongoing thought-based chatter in our heads, giving us greater opportunity to tune in to the present moment. For people in recovery, practicing meditation is highly recommended.

One of the main reasons that meditation has been around for over 2,500 years is that, in essence, it's extremely simple. The purpose of meditation is to set aside the distractions that constantly clamor for our time and attention, and consciously slow down our mind—starting with our thoughts—to bring us to this moment, here and now. Meditation provides a wide range of important health benefits. There are many ways to meditate and it's important to find an approach that fits for you. Refer to Pathways to Recovery for more in-depth information on meditation and its various benefits.

A Continuing Journey

As is the case with any major process of change, making progress in recovery—whether for you or your addicted loved one—usually takes the form of two steps forward, one step back. Your addicted loved ones find recovery in their own way and in their own time.

Sometimes, they never find their way to recovery. As tragic as that is, you can still engage in a process of learning, growth, and healing that will allow you to feel worthy and worthwhile, and give your life meaning and value. You can know with certainty that you are not alone; that there are many who have been through the same experiences and have become stronger as a result; and that support is available to you. Whatever happens, your addicted loved one will continue to be responsible for his or her own life and recovery, as you will continue to be responsible for yours.

If and when your addicted loved one enters professional treatment and/or begins to participate in a twelve-step or other recovery support program, by all means, support his or her involvement. While maintaining your own commitment to becoming healthy, it's important to show that you continue to be concerned about his or her successful long-term recovery. But, independent of what your addicted loved one does or doesn't do, it's helpful to keep in mind your commitment to the recovery process is also a commitment to the overall well being of yourself and your family as a whole.

Recovery is an ongoing process of shifting the way we think, modifying how we respond to our emotions, tuning in to and improving our physical well-being, and further developing our spirituality. These changes can help us make meaningful improvements in virtually all aspects of lives, including our relationships—within our family, with others, and with ourselves.

NOTES